JUST JEN

JUST JEN
Thriving Through Multiple Sclerosis

JEN POWLEY

Roseway Publishing
an imprint of Fernwood Publishing
Halifax & Winnipeg

Editing: Brenda Conroy
Cover Design: Tania Craan
Printed and bound in Canada

Published by Roseway Publishing
an imprint of Fernwood Publishing
32 Oceanvista Lane, Black Point, Nova Scotia, B0J 1B0
and 748 Broadway Avenue, Winnipeg, Manitoba, R3G 0X3
www.fernwoodpublishing.ca/roseway

Fernwood Publishing Company Limited gratefully acknowledges the
financial support of the Government of Canada through the Canada
Book Fund, the Manitoba Department of Culture, Heritage and
Tourism under the Manitoba Publishers Marketing Assistance Program,
the Province of Manitoba, through the Book Publishing Tax Credit,
the support of the Province of Nova Scotia
through the Department of Communities, Culture and Heritage
and the support of the Canada Council for the Arts.

Library and Archives Canada Cataloguing in Publication

Powley, Jen, 1977-, author
Just Jen : thriving through multiple sclerosis / Jen Powley.

Issued in print and electronic formats.
ISBN 978-1-55266-923-5 (softcover).--ISBN 978-1-55266-924-2
(EPUB).--
ISBN 978-1-55266-925-9 (Kindle)

1. Powley, Jen, 1977-. 2. Multiple sclerosis--Patients--Canada--
Biography. I. Title.

RC377.P69 2017   362.196'8340092
               C2016-908079-X
               C2016-908080-3

CONTENTS

THANK-YOUS

I ACKNOWLEDGE MY WONDERFUL family for making this project a reality — my mother, Barb Morris, and father, Bill Powley, especially. My grandmother and late grandfather, late stepfather, sister Nicole and her husband Danny, sister Candice and her husband Matt, stepsister Annette and her husband Danny, stepbrother James and his wife Kristi are all notable figures in my growth and development. I also want to acknowledge my mother's partner Joe Moyneur, who provides my mother with comfort and companionship. My friends from elementary and high school and university, such as Kristina, Dale and Annette, helped shape me into the person I am.

I thank my roommates past and current, who keep me laughing and remind me that the world isn't such a bad place. A huge thank you to all of my assistants, some of whom were mentioned and some of whom were not — all hold a special place in my heart. I got along with some of them better than others, but all of them gave me an appreciation for the different ways one can look at the world.

I acknowledge all the friends, neighbours and colleagues I worked with who impacted my values and my judgment. They taught me that having a disability does not stand in the way of having fun and enjoying new experiences. Thank you to the MS Society of Canada for their help with researching the possible connection between eating disorders and Multiple Sclerosis.

I especially thank Lorri Neilsen Glenn, Stephen Kimber and the students and mentors in the MFA program at the University of King's College for supporting me as I made this memoir a reality.

*"Any coward can fight a battle when he's sure of winning; but
give me the man who has pluck to fight
when he's sure of losing."*
— George Eliot

For Tom
and my mom

A NOTE ON
MY PROCESS

Technology has advanced so that voice recognition programs are readily available — perfect for a quadriplegic. But voice recognition software for a voice that changes throughout the day is not yet developed — a problem for a woman with advanced, progressive multiple sclerosis. After spending hours with programs like Dragon Naturally Speaking and not being able to activate my Motorola cellphone with a stern "OK Google," I gave up on off-the-shelf technical aids. In the United States, Motorola has a program where a cell phone can learn a person's unique voice, but it is not available yet in Canada. People work better. I write through an assistant. I dictate, he or she types and then reads it back to ensure my thoughts have been captured. The process is long and tedious. Editing is longer still. But I achieve my goal. I write better with some assistants than others. I long ago learned not to fight it but to allow each assistant's strengths to guide the contribution for that day. A different assistant will work the next day or that evening. I can hold on to a gem I want to write about for that long.

I wrote this memoir as factual. I relied on memory but backed up the memories with research. Some names and details were changed if I thought leaving them in their natural state might harm a person's reputation or if the individual asked not to be identified.

CRIPS

WHEN MILES FIRST SLEPT with me, I had already begun using a manual wheelchair. In those days, we used to lie on the couch in the apartment he'd asked me to share with him — he had left his walk-up for a wheelchair-accessible unit. He cradled me against his soft, black turtleneck as I cried on his shoulder, "I'm going to get worse."

I had been diagnosed with multiple sclerosis eight years earlier, when I was fifteen.

"I know. We'll fight it together." He was my first real partner.

Months later he began complaining about my work as a volunteer for a disability rights organization. "Why do you have to spend all your time on disability issues?"

"Someone needs to fight for equality."

"Can't you do normal work? Why do you always have to be around crips?" the man I moved across the country to be with pronounced.

"DON'T STOP THERE," MILES barked.

"Where *should* I stop?"

With great effort, I was slowly wheeling myself through the dense green mat of lawn to watch the Bengal Lancers Horse Show, near Halifax's Citadel Hill.

"The other crips are parked over there," he said, gesturing to the left with his head. "If we park there, people will think you're one of them."

Not wheelchair users but *crips*. Lame horses ready to be taken out to pasture.

I looked at him. He didn't look back.

"Then they'll think I'm either your father or a pervert."

Miles was seventeen years older than me, but we were both consenting adults. He didn't have a problem with my disability when we lay in bed together.

I realized that parking with the other wheelchairs was about him. He thought other people would judge him because he was dating a woman with a disability, or think he couldn't attract an able-bodied woman.

I felt second rate. In my university anthropology class we studied what made humans different from other primates. Humans could walk upright. If I couldn't walk, I must be less than fully human.

Three years later, I saw how other people saw me as I wheeled down the hallway of the Bloomfield Centre, an old school converted into a community space in North End Halifax, where I worked for a disability support organization. I turned the corner, steering the chair toward the washroom. As I passed by her, a woman in a wheelchair announced, "Multiple sclerosis."

It wasn't a question.

I felt diminished. I'd always been Jen. Just Jen. Now other people saw my disability before they saw me. If they continued to look, they might see Jen. But that woman didn't need a name — a diagnosis was enough.

DIAGNOSIS

LOOKING BACK AT THE events of my diagnosis from the age of thirty-eight, I remember details differently than my mother does. Mom remembers a four-hour trip from our home in Vegreville to the Southern Alberta Jubilee Auditorium in Calgary to watch *The Phantom of the Opera*. She vibrates with excitement as she talks about the performance of her favourite musical. I remember the same trip: fog so thick that my stepdad, Jim, drove home from Calgary with his door open so he could see the white line on the asphalt.

That evening, a couple of fingers on my left hand were numb. It wasn't the first time this had happened. They were colourless instead of their usual rosy pink. After Jim had safely brought us home, Mom went off to the library to do some research. Mom discovered that numb fingers are associated with a host of conditions, including pinched nerves, carpal tunnel syndrome, peripheral neuropathy and multiple sclerosis.

My concerns had begun with the loss of my ability to succeed in sport. A week earlier, at track practice, we were running through the hallways of Vegreville Composite Junior/Senior High School because it was raining outside. The only obstacle was the janitor's pile of dust.

My track coach jogged up alongside me and said, "You have to strike the ground with your heels first."

Vegreville Composite Junior/Senior High School senior girls basketball team, 1994 (Jen is standing on the far left).

"What?" I stammered. I was confused. I never thought about running. I just ran.

"The first part of your foot to hit the ground should be your heel."

He jogged ahead, running past the cafeteria and the signs advertising french fries and fried rice. I was mystified. I thought I had been running on my heels, but I realized I was running on my tiptoes like a three-year-old.

Mom made an appointment for me with Dr. Toderovich, our family doctor, who had delivered me fifteen years earlier. After Mom described her concerns and I discussed my trouble running, he asked, "Would you mind if I watched you put on your pants?"

I was perplexed. I leaned against the wall for balance while I pulled up my jeans.

"Sit down on the examining table."

With both hands on the table for balance, I used the footstool to climb up. I looked at him. He was looking at his clipboard.

4

Jen tubing at Lac Santé, near Two Hills, AB, June 1998.
(photo courtesy of Laetitia de Witt)

"I think you either have a brain tumour or multiple sclerosis. I'll schedule an MRI so we can find out for sure."

Dr. Toderovich left the room, saying he'd be right back.

My mom and I waited in the small examination room. Neither of us said a word. The fluorescent lights hummed, but all I heard echoing through my mind was *brain tumour*. I would die a tragic death. It had the ring of a heart-wrenching romance — like the scene with Megan Follows in the dory, playing the Lily Maid, in the Anne of Green Gables miniseries.

To that point, my only experience with multiple sclerosis was through the yearly MS Readathon. I asked my neighbours to pledge ten cents for each book I read. I now think the Readathon is an appropriate fundraiser for a disease characterized by mobility impairment.

IN THE HOSPITAL, I lay on a skinny stretcher that rolled into a metal cylinder. During the MRI there was a lot of clanging. I breathed consciously to control my claustrophobia.

Mom and I waited for the results in the neurologist's grey waiting room. Once we were in his office, he showed us images of my brain on a backlit white board on his wall. He didn't take his eyes off the images while he delivered the news.

"Jen does have multiple sclerosis." He continued, "I don't like to deliver this news to someone so young, but ..."

But what?

I was fifteen years old. At the time, that was considered young for a diagnosis. Multiple sclerosis was usually diagnosed between ages twenty and forty. Improvements in diagnostic technology since then have shifted the average age to between fifteen and thirty-five.

Mom and I were shuffled to an adjoining office to see a nurse for after-diagnosis care. My mom asked one question: "Can she still have kids?"

Kids?

First described by French physician Dr. Jean-Martin Charcot in 1868, multiple sclerosis is a neurological disease characterized by the demyelination of nerves. Demyelination removes the insulation around the nerve fibre. Like with bare wire, this short-circuits the body's electrical system. The brain sends messages but they do not arrive at their intended destination. Like travelling on a city street and being stopped by barricades, messages travelling the spinal cord are blocked by hard plaques, a type of scar tissue that replaces missing myelin. Multiple sclerosis sometimes demyelinates nerves in the brain itself. The disease may cause any variation of impaired balance, vision loss, memory problems, altered sensation and fatigue.

Some kinds of multiple sclerosis are characterized by debilitating episodes followed by a return to normal or near-normal functioning, some kinds cause a steady decline, and others are a combination of the two. Mom assumed I would have the same kind of multiple sclerosis as my friend's aunt, the relapsing-remitting type. She worked, and raised her kids, but needed to be careful not to exhaust herself.

I was a bit disappointed it wasn't a tumour. I could romanticize a tumour — tumours sounded sexy. Multiple sclerosis sounded shameful. It was as though something evil lurked inside me that one day would rear its ugly head. I tried to reason with myself. I could deal with this. Lots of people have multiple sclerosis. It's bad, but there are worse diseases. I could have lung cancer or HIV.

My specialist prescribed strong steroids, and I was able to manage life as usual. I was on prednisone at ten times the dosage my bodybuilding stepbrother was taking. It made my bones more porous and led me to put on forty pounds. I put on so much weight so fast I had stretch marks on my thighs.

I didn't tell anyone at school about my diagnosis, but I lived in a small town and people talked, so I knew everyone knew. I did write about it in a confidential journal for a class assignment. My teacher didn't break the confidentiality agreement so never spoke to me about it.

HEELS

"Why don't you just wear flats?" asked my mother.

"Why? Because it's my graduation. I already have a cocktail-length dress when all the other girls will be wearing full-length. How much of a freak do you want me to be?"

I didn't want a froofy ankle-length dress. My next-door neighbour's dress shop had a cranberry-coloured bodice I adored, so my neighbour sewed a cranberry, knee-length, chiffon skirt. I had a matching chiffon scarf and elbow-length gloves to complete the outfit.

"Calm down. We'll find you some low heels we can dye to match your dress."

I wasn't steady on my feet even in high-top sneakers. When I walked through the halls of my high school I would bounce from wall to wall for support — my friends called me Pinball. Not falling during an evening in heels was unlikely, but all my friends were wearing stilettos or four-inch platforms. I wanted to look like everyone else.

I bought a pair of shoes at a mall in Edmonton. They were dyed to match my dress. As soon as my stepdad brought them home, they went on my feet. I knew I had to practise walking in them. For the next week I walked up and down the spiral staircase in the living room. It was as close to the staircase in the gymnasium as I could find. One difference was that the stairs at home had a

8

handrail. I used the handrail for the first couple days, then I trained myself to do the stairs without it.

The program for graduation night featured the valedictorian address, then the handing out of diplomas. As we were called onto the stage, the vice-principal read our plans for after graduation: I had applied to physiotherapy at the University of Alberta.

To be accepted into the program my grades needed to be stellar and I needed to ace the interview. Half of the students were chosen out of high school, the other half were already in university. The interview was a blur but I remember crying. They asked me why I wanted to be a physiotherapist. Rather than stick with my prepared answer about wanting to work with

Friend Dale Osadchuk and Jen in Jen's living room prior to high school graduation ceremony, May 1995.

elite athletes, I broke down and told them about my multiple sclerosis and how I wanted to succeed in spite of my limitations.

After I picked up my diploma, I was expected to descend the eight-stair curved staircase from the height of the stage to the gym floor, unassisted. The staircase had handrails covered in black- and wine-coloured balloons and twisted crepe paper. I paused at the top of the stairs. The audience probably assumed I was being dramatic but what I was really doing was saying a little prayer. If I fell on these stairs at this moment, my high school experience would be in shambles. It wouldn't matter what I had achieved — everyone would remember my fall.

My practice sessions at home were not always graceful, but that night my friends weren't all graceful either. Their shoes were as alien to them as mine were to me. The only difference was the height of the heels. Their heels were higher than my quarter-inch kitten heels, but they didn't have a progressive neurological disease. They all managed to walk down the stairs — so would I. Though I felt a stumble, my parents said I managed to descend the stairs more or less gracefully. Maybe it was adrenaline. Maybe God answered my prayers.

NEVER GONNA
DANCE AGAIN

As a kid, I spent hours dancing along to John Weldon's vignette *The Log Driver's Waltz*. The animated television short showed the quick-stepping log driver as the true love of a small-town girl. I wanted to be that woman, twirling with her log driver.

My hometown of Vegreville, Alberta, had 5,000 residents. Largely a farming community, it hosted the annual Pysanka Festival. In the 1980s it had the largest youth competition of Ukrainian music and dance in Canada. I won my first medal there, at the age of six, for reciting a Ukrainian poem about a mouse. Every year after that I competed in some way or another until, at sixteen, multiple sclerosis impaired my balance, stripping me of my ability to participate. For two years, I couldn't go near the festival grounds. I couldn't venture to the grandstand music and dance performances with my grandmother. I couldn't bring myself to visit the beer tent. I boycotted the entire event. The strains of dulcimer music brought tears to my eyes.

I had begun ballet at the age of four, adding Ukrainian dancing to my repertoire at the age of twelve because I wanted to dance with a group rather than practising alone in the mirror. I thought of myself as a dancer. I wanted to move to the beat, picking up my feet in time to the rhythm, but now I couldn't.

After I could no longer spot my turns during dance practice, I tried karate, spending three nights a week at the dojo. When

Promin Ukrainian dance group after winning medal at dance competition in North Battleford, SK, in April 1993 (Jen is third from right).

balancing during the kicks in karate became impossible, I began swimming lengths. I wanted to feel the stretch of my tendons and the fatigue that comes from muscle exertion. My mother had instilled in me a need to be active. I just had to satisfy that need with something I could actually do. Maybe the activity I could do wasn't what I truly desired, but I was willing to negotiate with my multiple sclerosis. The disease could have the dancing and the karate. I would do something else.

I adored the rush of water on my face. I loved the resistance. I spent endless hours in the lake during our summer vacations — swimming, skiing and tubing. Swimming was something I could pursue without the eyes of the world on me. In the water I was safe. In the water I could cry and no one would know.

ONE SUMMER MORNING I woke at six and drove my grey Chevy Nova to the community recreation centre in Vegreville. The cash register stood alone, locked behind the steel security window. At that hour patrons paid the lifeguard directly.

I threw my clothes into one of the orange steel lockers. The smell of chlorine filled my nostrils. I didn't bother locking up my stuff even though it included my car keys and wallet. No thief would get out of bed at this hour. I took a quick shower. The cold water stung my skin. I looked back at my wet footprints on the terra cotta tiles as I walked from the change room to the pool. I ran my hand along the wall for balance. When the wall ended, I tottered to the edge of the pool, a distance of three steps in the open. If I crossed in the right place, I could grab the aluminium rail above the ladder to the deep end.

I dove in. The rush of water obliterated the harsh fluorescent lighting and the cheesy radio music.

Freedom.

No more balancing.

No more counting steps.

I could splash. I could turn. In the water, I could dance.

As I swam on my back, guided by the orange support beams on the ceiling, the outside world reappeared. I heard the saxophone strains of "Careless Whisper" through the pool's overhead speakers. I heard George Michael croon, "I'm never gonna dance again."

CHANGING COURSE

"ARE YOU OKAY?" THE old man asked me. Staring at me with glassy eyes and a pallid complexion, the man looked like he should be in the hospital across the street.

"I'm fine."

I flipped from my back to my knees. My backpack, like a turtle shell, had made the turn to uprightness difficult.

"I just slipped. I'll be fine."

I brushed the dirt and ice off my knees.

Damn it. That hurt.

I could feel the road rash on my knees. I hoped the blood wouldn't stain my jeans. My elbow was even more tender. I checked for blood as soon as I got to a washroom in the University of Alberta Hospital. The injured skin on my elbow stuck to my blue and green Faculty of Rehabilitation Medicine fleece jacket. At least the fleece had absorbed the blood. I pulled it away. A searing pain shot up my arm.

Damn it. Pull yourself together, Jen.

I didn't need this. I had a neurology exam in fifteen minutes.

A block away, I pulled open a door to the imposing Corbett Hall, home of the Faculty of Rehabilitation Medicine. Dragging my toes on the carpet, I trudged to the main hallway, where my classmates were waiting. Kevin was sitting on the floor, consuming his usual cheese and strawberry jam sandwich. One day I would work up the courage to try that combo. I turned down the hallway and joined a group of women who were cramming.

"What does cranial nerve number twelve do?" Judy asked.

Allison answered, "It's the hypoglossal nerve. The one that enervates the tongue."

These students were smart and coordinated. I knew the exam material too but felt distanced from them. What would they think of me if they knew about my multiple sclerosis?

After returning from my first placement, held during the winter semester of the first year of my physiotherapy degree, the program's clinical coordinator, Joan Loomis, said she wanted to meet with me. Once we were both settled in her office, she broke the news that my placement supervisor didn't trust me with clients. She thought it was risky for me to work hands-on because of my impaired balance. She suggested I focus on research.

I knew that what the clinical coordinator said was true. I didn't have enough balance. I couldn't stay and watch my classmates fulfil their dreams — my dream — if I knew I would only do research. At the end of the term, I transferred out of the physiotherapy program without saying farewell.

IN THE STREET LAMP's yellow light, snowflakes fell gently. I amused myself by creating shapes with my footprints in the fresh snow as I waited for my sister to pick me up after my anthropology class. Heel to toe, heel to toe. It was the last time I remember laying down footprints. The snow deadened all sound. The city faded away in the blackness. Technically, I was taking a year off on the recommendation of my neurologist, but had enrolled in two University of Alberta courses: anthropology and intro occupational therapy. The Faculty of Rehabilitation Medicine had been willing to let me transfer into occupational therapy. I had a class in the same building as physiotherapy, but I didn't look for any of my friends. My life moved forward. I wasn't where I used to be.

Jen at a family wedding, August 1998.

I THINK IT IS likely easier to become a quadriplegic in an automobile accident than through multiple sclerosis. It's less painful to cannonball into cold water than to wade in slowly. Disability works the same way. If I had an accident and was admitted to the hospital, it would be followed up with training at the rehabilitation centre: I would be taught how to dress, use a chair, and what adaptive equipment I needed. With multiple sclerosis, I was left to figure it out alone.

A research article published in the *Annals of Neurology* notes that ninety percent of patients with exacerbating or progressive conditions, like multiple sclerosis, show emotional disturbances, versus twelve percent of people in the spinal cord injuries control group. If a spinal cord injury had made me a quadriplegic, I wouldn't have had the chance to thank my toes for their hard work before their use was terminated, but I would only have had to adapt once. My abilities might have been taken in a flash, but that would have been the only flash to adapt to. With multiple sclerosis, I am constantly saying goodbye to my abilities.

FAITH

After my "year off" I attended King's University College in Edmonton, not because of its Christian outlook but because of its small campus. All the classes and the dormitory were in one building. The campus was formerly a hotel and convention centre. With the harsh Alberta winters and the progress of my multiple sclerosis, it was prudent to avoid long distances, snow and ice — these nearly killed me at the University of Alberta.

I asked the registrar, "Is it a problem if I'm not Christian?"

"You can make Christianity part of your stay with us but it is not required."

I had grown up in the Christian church but I hardly had a relationship with God. I never read the Bible, and I only prayed in church. When I was sixteen I had a falling out with the pastor's wife, who I had been teaching vacation bible school with. At snack time, I put the plate of cookies in the middle of the table. I figured most kids didn't really want to be spending their summer at church, and they should be allowed as many cookies as they wanted. She disagreed and wanted the plate passed around in an orderly manner with each kid limited to one cookie. Her attitude made me think Christianity was more about rules than compassion.

THE ORANGE LIGHT OF the setting sun filled my fourth-floor dorm room. I was sobbing, my head buried in my pillow. Why me? Why this disease? I was trying to understand how an all-powerful and loving God could have given me multiple sclerosis.

There was a soft knock on my door. My floormate Rhonda invited me to a devotional in her room. There would be prayer, bible verses and tea.

Rhonda must have seen my swollen eyes and tear-streaked face. She said with great certainty, "I'll pray for you."

I thanked her, closed the door and muttered, "It's your fucking God who did this to me. I don't want your prayers."

WHEN PROFESSOR JOHN MCTAGGART strode into the lecture hall, I knew he was a Christian. At King's all profs were required to sign a statement of faith. He looked more like a J. Crew ad than a professor. He wore the khaki cargo shorts and brown hiking boots of a mountaineer — a God-fearing mountaineer. He had straight blonde hair, cut to mid-ear, which he repeatedly pushed back. I took several of his sociology courses, partly because he asked deep questions, partly to get lost in his blue eyes.

I made routine trips down the brown-carpeted hallway to his office under the guise of discussing social theorists. One afternoon his battered hockey skates sat on his desk, ready for an afternoon of gliding on the frozen river. I asked him why I only got a nine out of ten on my last assignment.

"Jen, you understand the concepts but you could have done better," he said. "I expect more of you. I don't know why you want a ten. You're the best student in the class. You know that. Why do grades matter so much?"

"Grades matter because that way I know I'm doing okay."

"Of course you're doing fine. You're an intelligent young woman. You're what, eighteen? Nineteen?"

"Nineteen," I answered.

"So why does it matter what you got on the paper?"

I paused.

"Because my body is failing."

"I noticed you have a bit of a limp."

"I have multiple sclerosis." He turned to face me as I continued, "I have a hard time believing in a kind and loving God."

I hadn't planned to confide in Professor McTaggart. Considering how badly I wanted his validation, why would I expose something so vile about myself?

He cut the conversation short. Frozen water called him. My ruminations about how a higher power could sit back and watch me suffer weren't his priority. Frustrated, I left his office and headed down the long hallway.

Several hours later, there was a rap on my door. I didn't want to deal with Rhonda and another prayer meeting, but I answered anyhow. The bluish fluorescent light silhouetted Professor McTaggart. I invited him in, closing the door behind him. He handed me a book. Because of my waning eyesight (multiple sclerosis can affect the eyes), I had to bring it up to my face to read the title: *Man's Search for Meaning* by Viktor Frankl, a Holocaust survivor. My first reaction was glee that Professor McTaggart cared enough to bring me a book. My second was: I would rather have a hug. My third was: how can I relate to a Holocaust survivor?

Professor McTaggart had listened to my anguish. He didn't want to respond with platitudes. The author of the book he gave me didn't ask, "Why was I sent to the concentration camp?" but instead he asked, "Why shouldn't I have been sent?" Without a word, my professor challenged me to stop asking "Why me?" and instead ask, "Why *not* me?"

Why did I presume that I should not have to suffer? Were the other people in the world better candidates for suffering? Turning the "Why me" question on its head made me wonder whether I had some quality that put me above suffering. I couldn't think of any reason I should not suffer. I had a supportive family. I was probably a better candidate for suffering than someone without the support and the abilities I had been given.

A TRAY
FULL OF FOOD

THE LAYOUT OF MY dorm was mapped in my head. I knew how many paces it was from my bed to the bureau, from the bureau to the bathroom door, from there to the toilet, from the toilet to the front door, from the front door to the elevator, from the elevator to the security door, from the security door to the cafeteria. I lived my life by counting steps, by calculating whether I had enough energy and enough desire to move from one spot to the next. Once I arrived at my destination the challenge only increased.

The cafeteria was the most difficult. Students were expected to carry a tray full of food (usually hot), accompanied by a beverage, across an open space to a table. We then had to navigate between the tables, lift the tray over the heads of seated people, and place the tray on the table without spilling. Impossible. I ate a lot of apples and dinner buns — neither required a tray. The worst that happened when I dropped them was a bruised apple or a bun with a smudge of floor grease. I could handle that. What I could not deal with was the embarrassment of broken dishes or spilt milk. I would not eat if it required embarrassment.

On a day like any other, I stood in front of the hot meal counter. I made eye contact with the short-order cook, Scott. He asked, "What can I get you?"

The aroma of ginger enticed me toward food with an Eastern flavour. I wanted to order a vegetable stir-fry and finish it with a healthy dose of soya sauce, but I knew the stir-fry came on a plate with a bed of rice. If I spilled it, the mess would attract attention. I didn't want my schoolmates to see that I was less able than they were. Scott also worked the cash because the cafeteria was small. If I asked him, I bet he would carry the plate of stir-fry to the table for me. But there would be questions. I couldn't deal with questions.

I walked past the grill and grabbed an apple from the basket of fruit by the cash register.

BECAUSE OF A BOYHOOD bout of rheumatic fever and a later battle with arthritis, my grandfather had a hard time walking from his chair in the living room to the dining room table, where we had family meals. He wouldn't use a cane around his acquaintances in Vegreville, but he used one in Edmonton, where he had the comfort of anonymity. He used Grandma as his cane at local gatherings and family weddings. He was ashamed of being less than perfect.

Grandma had a different attitude. Though her back was stooped, her feet shuffling, and she'd had her share of falls in the garden and on the stairs, she used her cane to cover the three-house distance to the community mailbox to pick up her mail. She had a walker ready for when she needed it, but confidently declared she didn't need it yet and wouldn't use it until she did.

Though frightened of losing her mobility, she accepted it as part of aging. But it was hard for her to see her twenty-year-old granddaughter struggling.

A PICKLE
ON THE SIDE

EVERY SUNDAY, AFTER MY therapeutic horse-riding lesson, my mother and I stopped for lunch at the Artisan Café on Whyte Avenue in Edmonton. Seating ourselves at a table for two, we waited for our orders to be taken.

"Can I get a grilled cheese panini with a pickle on the side?"

Mom ordered something with meat. After we ate, Mom snuck off to the washroom. I took it as an opportunity to flirt with the cute guy who made the sandwiches.

"Could I get an extra pickle?" I asked.

He smiled and handed me an extra large pickle. I took it to mean he was flirting right back.

"Would you consider going on a date?"

This was the first guy I had ever asked out. I hoped my request for a pickle didn't give him the wrong idea — not that I wasn't open to that.

We met a week later. It was awkward. He didn't ask any questions about why I used a cane. Maybe he understood disability; he had a hearing problem and his speech was unclear. We talked more about my university and his hopes of attending technical school. When the evening ended there was no kiss. He told me he was moving to British Columbia. He didn't offer his new address, nor did he ask for mine.

It was my only date during the five years of my undergrad program.

Since I wasn't having much luck with men, I thought maybe I should try women. I thought women were more compassionate than men. In western society, women are traditionally socialized to be caregivers and nurturers. Maybe the fact that I had multiple sclerosis wouldn't make me untouchable in the eyes of a woman.

I edited my small university's newspaper. One Tuesday night as I laid out that week's copy at the desktop computer, I watched my assistant editor approach the office. I heard the main door of the former cold beer store jangle open and the clomp of feet stomping snow from boots. Her cheeks were rosy from her short walk in the January evening. Half my mind was listening to her ramblings about the paper; the other half was examining the curves in her navy polo shirt. I mumbled a response.

"Are you going to be here late today?" she asked.

"Probably all night, like usual."

I hoped she understood the invitation to join me. We could make out on the worn sofa.

"I don't know how you do the all-nighters," she said. "I'll be back bright and early, but I need to put my head against a pillow."

I was curious how a woman would react to my touch. I appreciated the soft edges of the female body, the appeal of a woman's sweet breath.

I imagined my small breast within her wide mouth, her lips gently enveloping my firm nipple. I could picture her blue eyes looking up from between my knees. I could love a woman and maybe a woman would accept me despite the fact that I was damaged.

I never acted on my thoughts. Maybe it was my small town Alberta heritage, maybe it was that I was living in a Christian-reformed educational setting, or maybe I was just scared.

MY FIRST
WHEELCHAIR

"JEN, DO YOU WANT to come on the cruise?" asked my older sister, Nicole.

A year after Nicole graduated from the University of Alberta with her bachelor of science, she planned a Mediterranean cruise with her best friend and her best friend's husband. He worked for Air Canada and received a special deal with Holland America Line. Holland America had a doctor on board, so my medical worries were waylaid.

"There is one condition," she said. "You have to use a wheelchair."

I had been fighting against using a wheelchair. I had given into using a cane only six months earlier. Even then, I only used the cane sporadically.

People who succeeded in fighting multiple sclerosis didn't have to use a wheelchair. People would know that I wasn't trying hard enough. I couldn't push off from my toes when I walked and instead took a step by lifting my hip. Sometimes my toes would catch on the concrete. I would fall and scrape my palms but I could shake it off. The scuffs on my shoes were the only lasting damage.

For five years, I pursued alternative treatments. I tried acupuncture and vitamins. I rubbed emu oil on my legs. I tried methotrexate (a cancer drug). I tried prednisone (a steroid). On the recommendation of an acupuncturist I eliminated meat, gluten, dairy, tomatoes and citrus from my diet. I exercised daily: swam three

Dan Lake carrying Jen down a flight of stairs in Athens, Greece, May 1999.

times a week, did six flights of stairs on the off days. I stretched every morning. None of it helped.

Looking at the places I would go on the cruise — Turkey, Greece, Malta, Spain, Portugal, France and England — I rethought my initial *no*. I asked Nicole, "Can I take a few days to think about it?"

Why should I let the stares I fear prevent me from having a once-in-a-lifetime experience? No one on the trip — except for Nicole, Karen and Dan — would ever see me again, and I rationalized that it would be alright to use a wheelchair if it was a nice-looking, sporty wheelchair, not a hospital-issue monstrosity. I decided to go.

Old Europe was not built with wheelchairs in mind. When we came to somewhere the chair couldn't travel, Dan, who worked as a baggage handler and a teacher, would bend over, put one arm under my knees, the other under my arm and around my back, and lift with a cheerful "Alley-oop."

While Dan carried me, his wife, Karen, hefted my thirty-pound solid-frame wheelchair on her back, elbows out in front. She never complained, though her load was the most troublesome. My sister, the smallest of the group, carried the packages and bags we took on our daytrips.

The stairways to the basement bathrooms were sometimes too narrow for Dan to carry me. When I needed to pee I had to find the strength to venture down the stairs myself. If I couldn't, I relied on the sanitary napkins I wore to catch the dribbles.

We got a few funny looks, but no one asked questions. Anonymity lessened my shame.

One day, they carried me up the stairs to the observation deck aboard the MS *Amsterdam*, our cruise ship, and left me to explore for half an hour. The blue water of the Mediterranean surrounded us and bright sunlight highlighted the Rock of Gibraltar.

"Beautiful, isn't it?" said a good-looking middle-aged man.

A well-manicured woman standing next to him continued, "The sunlight is so white."

I agreed with them both and asked where they were from.

"Sorry to ask, but how are you going to get down?" said the man, who was an airline pilot from Florida.

"My friend brought me up. He'll be back to take me down."

"I could carry you down if you need," the pilot offered.

"He'll be back in half an hour. He wanted me to have some time by myself, but thank you."

The couple looked sceptical, so I wheeled away. I didn't know whether to be flattered by his concern, or annoyed that he thought I was so inept that I wouldn't consider how I was going to get off the deck. Did the couple feel sorry for me?

I feared their pity. It connotes an imbalance of power. It is not empathy, but condescension. English balladeer and civil rights activist Johnny Crescendo coined the phrase "Piss on pity!" I don't want anyone's goodwill because my legs don't work. I want their respect because my brain does.

Dan and Karen returned in half an hour to carry me off the sundeck.

My sister and I took the obligatory photo with the captain to send to my father and grandmother. I refused to be in the wheelchair for the photo. Instead, I stood, sticking my butt out to compensate for my lack of balance. In the photo I do not look like a happy traveller. I look like I was in pain.

Although the wheelchair didn't eliminate every problem — I skipped out of going to the Blue Grotto in Malta because the path was rocky — it allowed me to navigate city streets and maintain my energy. Before the wheelchair, I was too tired to do anything once I reached my destination. I didn't swim while I was at the University of Alberta. I didn't have enough energy to walk the three blocks to the Butterdome, much less swim lengths.

While getting ready in our room for a day on the North Atlantic, I said, "Nicole, I'm taking my wheelchair to the pool."

"Your chair? What happened to calling it *the rental?*"

I wheeled myself to the Lido deck and swam my requisite number of lengths. Then I played bingo and went to an art show.

When we got home, I purchased the chair.

At the time, television news programs were following Rick Hansen on his Man in Motion World Tour. I was determined to become as cool as he was.

The tank tops I wore to show off my chest now showed off my burgeoning biceps. I trained going up the hill near my mother's house. It was a long, slow climb that worked my endurance. I didn't want bulging muscles. I wanted lean, defined muscles. I missed how I looked standing up, so I worked to look cool sitting down. I got sexy wheelchair gloves (actually mountain bike gloves). They provided better traction and made me look saucy.

My wheelchair didn't confine — it liberated.

Dr. John McTaggart and I became friends. The neurological chaos inside my frame didn't matter. My mind and my empathy were what mattered.

Not walking made it a challenge to achieve certain goals. My dream of mountain climbing had to change. When I was in high school, I had read an article about Peter Croft, a mountain climber who didn't use any ropes. To climb without ropes you had to know what every muscle's capability was. With multiple sclerosis

I couldn't trust my body. One day I could walk, and the next I couldn't.

John didn't climb, much less climb without ropes. He hiked, but he had the same assuredness I imagined Peter Croft had. Although my physical limits were changing, at least I could surround myself with people who were sure of theirs.

That summer, my mother and I stayed at a cabin in Peter Lougheed Provincial Park near Banff. The camp was constructed especially for wheelchair users, with paved trails and accessible units. We offered John a spot on our couch for the week we were there. As a thank-you he spent a day hiking with me. We took the gondola up Sulphur Mountain in Banff. For the first time, from the summit of that mountain, I really understood how certain shadows on the ground were cast by clouds. I realize I should have figured this out long before, but it was so visceral on that mountain.

Being with John in the mountains made me think that I could survive in a wheelchair. The things I could enjoy were different. I couldn't hike to the top of Sulphur Mountain but I could get there as long as I had a friend to push me and help with the transfer. My dreams did not have to die — they just needed to be reframed.

GET YOUR
OWN DISEASE

When I was in high school, my stepdad and I went to Shaw's Point, a campground on Lesser Slave Lake, to meet his two kids and their families for a fishing party. My mother had no interest in fishing. I hoped to intersperse water skiing with the fishing, so I was happy to go along.

As we got ready for bed the first night, Jim started to experience pain radiating down his arms. I knew enough first aid to recognize this as a classic sign of a heart attack. There was a hospital forty-five minutes away. I suggested we make a visit to the emergency department.

We pulled our twenty-seven-foot, twenty-year-old motorhome into the parking lot. The doctor looked him over and released him. This was his third trip in as many years to a hospital for radiating pain. Each time they released him but encouraged him to come back if it ever happened again.

Though eventually Jim succumbed to a heart attack, the pain was likely due to multiple sclerosis. He was diagnosed four years after I was.

Because we lived in the same house, ate the same food and used the same cleaning supplies, I thought environmental factors were likely the cause of our multiple sclerosis. Then, my biological father was diagnosed with multiple sclerosis. I had half his DNA, but we did not live in the same house, so the environmental factors were not shared. I began to think heredity was a likely cause for multiple sclerosis.

Though my stepdad's diagnosis caught me off guard, I saw my biological father's diagnosis coming. One afternoon we ventured to Edmonton's Legislature Grounds. I was in my first year of physiotherapy and had just finished a course on gait. I noticed Dad didn't push off from his right toe: he raised his right hip and swung his leg forward. His gait was reminiscent of my own. A scuffmark blemished his otherwise perfect black loafers. He was diagnosed with multiple sclerosis seven years later.

When I didn't understand what was happening with my body, I didn't have anyone to turn to. I had to figure out each new experience. My stepdad and father thought they could turn to me. After they were diagnosed, they asked endless questions. They wanted me to explain what was happening to them, or at least commiserate. I should have been more empathetic, but I was angry and uncomfortable. When did I stop being their daughter and become their multiple sclerosis expert?

Jim asked, "Do your clothes hurt your skin?" His flannel button-ups caused his skin to itch and burn.

"No. Maybe you should change your laundry detergent," I said. "I can't use Tide, maybe it's the same sort of thing for you."

Another day, he asked, "Can you work all day?" He found his balance was worse after lunch. He started having daily afternoon naps.

I replied, "I don't have a problem with fatigue. I can work all day."

Jim explained how he was having problems remembering details. He and my mother asked me about this. He had started writing everything down. I told him I didn't forget things.

My biological father asked more questions.

"I have to pee all the time and without much notice."

"You know about my bladder urgency — how I have had to stop twice to go to the bathroom on the way to Edmonton 100 kms away." He would have to talk details with his own doctor.

Dad asked, "Does heat bother you? I've been thinking about getting air conditioning for the office. I wanted to know if you thought that was a good idea."

"Do what you think is best."

ON MY OWN

MY SISTER ASKED MY mother, "Would you let Jen go to Nova Scotia if she weren't disabled?"

"Of course," replied my mother.

"Think about that."

Years earlier, I had asked Mom if I could go to school overseas.

"You wouldn't qualify for health insurance. Your multiple sclerosis would be a pre-existing condition." She continued, "Who do you know over there who would help you, anyhow?"

"I'll meet people."

When I lived in Alberta, she liked the fact that if I ever had a problem, she and my stepdad and my father were only a phone call away. They could be at my university residence in an hour. I hated that. I did not feel like I was on my own. If I had the slightest screw-up, they swooped in to rescue me.

A couple of university friends and I talked about continuing our education at Dalhousie in Halifax. One of those friends was Anne. She was smart and beautiful, the Rubenesque type that John McTaggart, who was then her boyfriend, was attracted to.

"We're going to go to Dalhousie," explained Anne. "It's as far away from here as you can get and still be in Canada."

I ached to say: actually Memorial University in St. John's, Newfoundland, is farther. But I held my tongue.

Mom couldn't object to me going to Nova Scotia because of

health coverage, but physical accessibility was an issue. Founded in 1749, Halifax was not as ancient as the European city I originally wanted to study in, but compared to Alberta it was old. This meant a large part of Halifax wasn't friendly to wheelchairs. Building accessibility codes only applied to new buildings or when there was a change in use. If a restaurant had always been a restaurant, it wasn't required to meet new accessibility standards.

My friends hadn't considered this. If I lived with them, we wouldn't be able to live in an old Victorian house with a sweeping balcony and a grand stairwell, the kind of place, I assumed, students wanted to live.

I told Anne, "You don't want me to go with you."

I shouldn't have worried about Anne. She didn't come to Halifax, nor did any other of my friends. By the end of that summer they had other dreams. Anne was engaged to John McTaggart.

I was accepted into journalism at the University of King's College in Halifax.

Mom had agreed to let me go to Nova Scotia, yet she refused to just put me on a plane and let me deal with moving to Halifax on my own. She came with me for the first two weeks, sleeping on an air mattress on my dorm room floor. The King's College dormitories weren't wheelchair accessible, so I stayed one block away at a Dalhousie residence that did have an accessible room.

During the two weeks she was in Halifax, Mom had meetings with a professor and a student services coordinator at Kings. They didn't say anything extraordinary, but they were genuine and competent. These conversations lessened her fears.

Mom trusted my ability to advocate for myself. Though she was reluctant to leave me, she knew she couldn't spend her life hovering. I had to navigate my own way.

PAT THE BUNNY

MY FRIEND'S THREE-YEAR-OLD BROTHER shook off attempts to help him with his coat.

"I do that," he'd say. He had just mastered buttons. Though his dexterity was still developing, his commitment to do it himself was admirable.

Months after they leave the womb, children discover their hands, curl and uncurl their fingers. A year after that, between thirteen and eighteen months, they figure out how to use utensils.

I was unlearning the skills I had once mastered.

Zippers became a problem. I could zip the fly of my jeans, but small zippers, like those on wallets, were impossible.

Velcro closures on shoes reminded me of elementary school. I was not willing to shed all appearances of maturity for convenience. I resorted to elastic laces I kept tied. Under close inspection you could see the difference, but people on the street wouldn't notice.

I gave up shirts with buttons the year I moved to Halifax. The impossibility of manipulating tiny buttons into their holes was frustrating.

I had read *Mine for Keeps*, Canadian author Jean Little's novel about a girl with cerebral palsy, when I was ten. Sally, the heroine, left a segregated school for students with disabilities to return to her family's home. Sally's mother bought clothes that would be easy for her to deal with. I admired Sally's courage and how accepting her family was of her differences. Her special needs weren't problems — they were merely challenges. My mother picked out clothes for me with the same care as Sally's mother.

I visited my sister's home in Edmonton when her firstborn, Maddie, was one year old. I parked my wheelchair at the kitchen table, careful to avoid wheeling over the tiny fingers of my crawling niece. I settled into a conversation with Mom, Nicole and Danny, my sister's husband. Maddie wasn't walking yet but she had learned to stand. After some catching up, I noticed Maddie clutching the spokes of my wheelchair tire. As I watched, she pulled herself to a stand.

She was comfortable.

My wheelchair didn't scare her — she saw it as an extension of me.

She didn't feel sorry for me.

I LEARNED TO APPLY mascara as a pre-teen. When my multiple sclerosis began to numb my hands, I couldn't put on mascara or put in contacts if I didn't want to poke an eye out. Certain tasks I preferred to give up rather than allow someone else to do them. Applying mascara was one of those. I dyed my eyelashes.

When I lost the big skills, like walking, it was hard, but the little losses were just as traumatic.

The year I moved to Halifax, seven years after being diagnosed, I reached into the front pocket of my black courier bag to get a stick of gum. I pulled out my hand to find it clenching a nail clipper. It should have been simple to distinguish between the cold, hard metal of the nail clipper and the paper wrapper of a Wrigley's Juicy Fruit. I had learned differences between textures from *Pat the Bunny,* by Dorothy Kunhardt, the touch-and-feel book, when I was two. I had learned about shapes from Fisher-Price block sets. Now with multiple sclerosis, the nerve-endings in my fingertips abandoned me. One texture, one shape, was equal to any other.

I had a single alcoholic drink while in the one-year journalism program in Halifax in 2001. My balance was so precarious that one drink was enough to throw off my coordination. I had a cranberry and vodka in the King's Wardroom before I went for bagels and cream cheese at the nearby Coburg Coffee House.

Once my friends and I arrived at the café, I went to the washroom. The washroom door was held closed by a hook-and-eye latch made of bent nails. I parked my chair perpendicular to the toilet and reached for the grab bar on the wall. I planted my grey North Face hikers firmly in front of the toilet, pulled myself to a stand, and pivoted. My ass hit the cold, firm toilet seat with a plunk. After I did my thing, I had to accomplish the reverse: pull myself to a stand with the grab bar, pull up my underwear and my jeans with one hand while maintaining my grip on the grab bar with the other. Pivot. Sit.

My knee gave out as I was pulling up my jeans.

Shit.

I tried to reach out with my butt so it would contact the seat of the wheelchair. No luck. My butt hit the bar where my feet went, twelve inches short of where I needed it.

Shit.

Silence.

Shit.

More silence.

Okay. I can do this. The grab bar is right there.

And then the chair started to roll backwards.

Now I wasn't in reach of the grab bar. There was no stall door to crawl under. I could call for help but that would signal defeat. If I did call for help, they would have to take the hinges off the door, which opened into the restaurant. I was worried the coffee shop staff would call the fire department or an ambulance, and everyone would see my predicament.

I could throw my shoe at the lock. If I threw it from the bottom up, it might unlatch the lock. The door would swing open and I would be rescued without the fire department having to show up. Great plan. I had managed to pull my underwear up, so at least I was decent. There had been times back in Alberta when I hadn't accomplished this. Thankfully, my rescuer had been my stepdad — I trust he didn't look at my scruffy bikini line. With college boys, I couldn't assume the same. I took my shoe off and threw it at the lock. I thought ring toss was hard, but this was impossible. It was harder still to slither after my shoes once I'd thrown them. It was futile to try to unlatch the door.

I had to pull myself up, get back on the toilet, and pull my chair closer. It could be done.

Toes of my boots against the wall, I leaned my shoulder against the front of the toilet bowl to reach the grab bar. On the count of three, I would pull myself to a stand, hoping my knees would lock.

One. Two. Restart.

Deep breath.

One. Two. Three.

A little *urgh* to get my muscles going — it works in karate.

You're standing. Okay. Stay calm. You need to turn your hips and fall onto the toilet. You can do this.

Okay. You're sitting. Rest up. Deep breath in.

Shimmy your jeans as far up as they will go. You need to eliminate as many tasks as you can from the time you will spend in a stand, but you don't want to rush.

Don't panic. You are as good as down if you do.

Breathe.

Breathe.

I managed to get my jeans up, sit in my chair, and unlock the door. I returned to my friends. They were done their coffees.

One of my friends asked, "What took you so long?"

"I don't feel well," I replied.

That was the only social event I went to that year. I didn't want to risk any more fiascos.

MEETING MILES

I HAD A WORKER from Red Cross Home Care walk me to the Bengal Lancers stable each Sunday morning. Home care provides housekeeping and personal care. It helps keep people out of nursing homes. At that time homecare workers could walk with clients to the mailbox or to buy groceries — or to the horse barn. The worker would push my manual wheelchair to the riding club while I gave directions.

One Sunday, my homecare worker called to say she had missed her bus because her daughter had broken a glass and she had to clean it up. She wouldn't make it in time for my lesson. I was not impressed. I called the barn.

"I won't be able to make it to class today."

"Where do you live?" asked the instructor.

"Howe Hall, the Dalhousie Residence, about ten minutes away, at the corner of Coburg and Lemarchant."

"I'll get a volunteer to pick you up."

That volunteer was Miles. He didn't have a wheelchair-accessible vehicle but he was strong enough to scoop me out of my chair and place me in his red four-by-four Jimmy. He threw the wheelchair into the back of the truck.

The therapeutic power of horses helps people with physical, emotional and intellectual disabilities. Each person takes something different from the experience of riding. For me, the movement of the horse relaxed my leg muscles and simulated the ambulation I used to perform. Depending on their level of balance, the rider has one or two side-walkers to ensure they don't slip off. Miles was my side-walker. Because my balance on the horse was quite good, I only had one. From my vantage point, I teased Miles about his growing bald spot.

Before he drove me home, I asked him if I could take him for lunch to thank him for his generosity. He agreed. We went to a local market and shared crepes. He was wearing a white and blue polo shirt with another button-up shirt beneath it. I thought the two collars looked awkward. My sister would have commented disparagingly on it — I let it slide.

The sun streamed through the windows. Miles talked to me about boats and the difference between starboard and port. We said we should hang out more often, and he gave me his phone number. I was elated. My hours of staring into the mirror wondering why I was unlovable seemed wasted.

Miles and I went to see *Quills*, starring Joaquin Phoenix, at a Cineplex that weekend. We didn't kiss during the movie. We waited until he dropped me off.

The weekend after that, he invited me to his place for supper and to watch the mockumentary *This Is Spinal Tap*, about a fake British rock band. His apartment wasn't wheelchair accessible so he carried me up the stairs and sat me on his couch. I don't remember what happened in the movie. My mind was elsewhere. He was thirty-nine and no doubt had been with other women. I was twenty-two and preoccupied with sex. Women in Canada lose their virginity at an average age of fifteen. I had never been with a man.

Soon, Miles and I were kissing. I was lying on my back. His hands were on my waist, under my sweater. He began unbuckling his belt. He wanted more. I wanted more.

"Miles, I'm a virgin."

I revealed my deep, dark secret. I thought it might bring an end to it all.

"So? It doesn't matter," he replied between kisses.

I was shocked that he didn't care.

"Do you want to stay over?" he asked.

I nodded.

"Jen, do you want to try living with me?" asked Miles. "Nothing permanent but just a trial."

We were hanging out in his apartment. He was marking papers for a course he taught at a local university. I was watching him from the couch. My mind exploded in jubilation. A guy had asked me to live with him! I yearned for this kind of commitment.

"You know I'm scheduled to move back to Alberta. I have a flight booked," I said. "But I would like to come back. I can break it to my parents in person. But Miles," I added, "I don't think I can stay in Nova Scotia unless it's a definite thing."

Miles held firm. "I don't think we should move in with each other without a trial."

"But don't you see why I can't stay unless it's the real thing?"

Eventually he capitulated, but I didn't acknowledge what he was really saying. He didn't want me for a life partner — he just wanted to try.

My stepdad picked me up from the Edmonton airport in his green Ford farm truck. His trusty dog, Jake, was in the back of the crew cab.

"I met a guy in Nova Scotia. He's asked me to live with him."

Jim was wearing shades to protect his eyes from the midday sun, so I couldn't read his expression.

I continued, "Can you break it to Mom?"

"Isn't that something you would rather tell her yourself?" he asked.

"No. You can break it to Mom gently. If *you* do it, she won't be as upset."

"I'll try," he said.

I remembered how hard I had fought to get her approval to go to school in Halifax. I thought moving in with a guy, all the way across the country, would be a much tougher sell. Eventually we talked about it. She understood that I wanted a relationship. Four months later I boarded a plane back to Halifax.

GROWING FRUSTRATION

I COULDN'T FIND A job, though I was trained as a journalist. At that time print journalists were in demand, but you had to be able to take your own photos and drive. I couldn't take photos. Even if I didn't blur the picture by jiggling the camera, my impaired eyesight made for dubious choices of subject: I might take a photo of what I thought was a woman working in a garden only to find out it was a scarecrow. I had given up my driver's licence because my vision made street and traffic lights indistinguishable and because I couldn't tell the difference between the pavement and the median. I had gone to school for eighteen years. I ought to be able to find a job. Miles was paying the rent and the grocery bills. I didn't want to be a kept woman. I wanted to contribute to our fledgling household.

I found employment as a secretary with the University of King's College Department of Journalism. I had graduated from there six months before so I knew the program and the people. The woman who had been the replacement for the secretary (who was receiving cancer treatment) was herself leaving for a "real job" with the CBC in British Columbia. I wished I had a real job.

Working at King's was interesting but not ideal. I always felt like I had to do things like the former secretary did things. Those ways weren't always viable for me. I felt like I didn't fit the bill. She had used a manual typewriter for filling in forms. The manual typewriter was on a ledge that I couldn't reach from my wheel-chair. I couldn't use the photocopier independently. It was too high. Other staff members were more than happy to help, but I didn't like to ask. They had their own jobs to do. The filing cabinets were also too high. I was good at getting the director's mail and organizing it in terms of priority on his desk. That was a small accomplishment.

There was a pair of the former secretary's shoes under the desk. I always felt like I should be filling those shoes, but my wheels didn't fit.

PEANUT BUTTER BALLS

"JEN, YOU'RE GETTING PRETTY skinny," Miles said.

"I'm fine," I snapped.

"It's like sleeping next to a skeleton."

I wanted to remind him of his increasing girth but thought better of it. He didn't deserve an answer.

A month earlier, Miles and I had made peanut butter balls — orbs of peanut butter, Rice Krispies and icing sugar. We made them small so I would eat them. I had started to be concerned with how much and what kind of food I consumed. I didn't want anything with fat in it. I steamed vegetables, never fried them.

"I dare you to eat three peanut butter balls," said Miles.

"All at once?" I replied.

"You bet."

I couldn't do it. I ate one but couldn't eat three. That would use up all my allocated calories for both that day and the next. I had already eaten what I deserved: half an apple, two plain rice cakes, a dried nectarine and two pieces of Dentine Ice chewing gum. I didn't have a "real" job so I didn't see myself as contributing to the world. If I were giving more to society, then I might deserve food. At the moment, I did not.

I would work off the calories from what I did consume through exercise. I had bought a variable resistance hand bike, the equivalent of a treadmill for wheelchair users. I told myself it was to strengthen my arm muscles and not primarily to burn off calories. What I told myself wasn't my real motivation.

Worried about my weight loss, Miles called my mother. Mom said to keep an eye on my eating and invited him to call again if he continued to be concerned. Miles urged me to go to the doctor about my eating problems. He came to the appointment because he didn't trust me to tell the doctor the real story.

Dr. Spicer, our family doctor, outlined what treatments were available in Halifax. "If you were overweight, there are many things I could do for you, but being underweight your options are limited. There are a couple of beds at the psychiatric hospital and there is a program that deals with outpatients with eating disorders. I'll get my secretary Janice to look them up and she'll call you with that information tomorrow. Or you could just eat a Tim Horton's bran muffin every day. That would help."

I chuckled at his joke, but knew there was no way I would eat a Tim Horton's muffin. For immediate assistance, Dr. Spicer referred me to a psychiatrist.

Between a quarter and half of all persons with multiple sclerosis deal with a major case of depression. I was no exception.

The way the psychiatrist gently bobbed her head with each answer I gave to the mood inventory test told me I was depressed. When asked, "Do you think your future is hopeless?" I answered, "Yes."

"Can you use the scale, please?" The psychiatrist had laid out a six-point scale for me to use when responding.

"Six." Always.

"Have you lost interest in aspects of your life that used to be important to you?"

"Yes."

Again, she pointed to the scale.

What I really wanted to say was: You know, your sport socks and running shoes look ridiculous with your dress pants.

I answered, "Six."

I wanted her approval more than I wanted to ridicule her.

She prescribed anti-depressants. I never took them. I was locked in a world of depression and felt I had to find the door myself. I did not want a pharmaceutical solution. I needed to do the headwork. Having multiple sclerosis was depressing — I knew my physical disability would only get worse. Not eating was something I was good at. It made me feel in control. My illness had taken away so much of my physical ability — something I had been very proud of when I was growing up. Not eating let me rule my body in the only way I could. Frustrated and concerned, Miles called Mom a second time. Mom travelled from Alberta to Halifax at Miles's request.

I know my experience of trying to gain control through food isn't unique. Two studies — one from Scotland, one from Turkey — suggest that eating disorders are more common in people with multiple sclerosis than in the average individual. Further study needs to be done.

Mum was shocked when she saw me. My cheekbones jutted out prominently, giving me an icy stare. She immediately started preparing dishes she thought would entice me to eat. She made a lentil vegetable stew. I was okay with eating vegetables because they were low in calories, but lentils?

"In many countries, lentils are what they feed cattle. You're certainly as worthy as a cow," Mom rationalized.

"In some countries, cows are sacred. I'm certainly not as deserving of reverence as they are."

I investigated the options Dr. Spicer had mentioned. Miles and I visited the inpatient unit at the psychiatric hospital for an assessment. As the nurse sat us down in the conference room, we heard a man hollering, "My leg! My leg! Someone took my leg!" I couldn't voluntarily be admitted to this unit.

My weight was too low to qualify for outpatient help in Halifax, where a patient needed a body mass index of eighteen. My BMI was barely sixteen. The cognitive behaviour therapy at the foundation of the outpatient program depended on patients' ability to think rationally. If your BMI ratio wasn't high enough, you likely didn't have the mental capacity required. I thought I was being perfectly reasonable because I was the one who was seeking treatment. I knew I had a problem.

Because I hadn't yet filed a Nova Scotia tax return I wasn't technically a resident. I decided to look at my options in Alberta. The University of Alberta hospital had an inpatient unit.

"You meet the criteria for the program," said the psychiatrist in charge. "Unfortunately, the rooms and washrooms in this unit aren't wheelchair accessible."

"But you'll take me?"

"If you can find somewhere else to stay, we would definitely take you." I could stay at my mother's house in Vegreville, one hour away from Edmonton.

Before I left Halifax I completed my contract with the University of King's College. I planned the former secretary's "retirement party." It was a thinly veiled pre-funeral gathering, her cancer having returned. After the party, Mom, still in Halifax, turned to me and said, "The cords in your neck stick out more than that dying woman's." She was hoping to convince me to eat.

Mum and I flew to Alberta, and I started the program. In order to make the eight o'clock breakfast at the eating disorder unit we had to be on the road from Vegreville at 6:30 every morning. I never divulged my inner thoughts to my dad or stepdad so we drove in silence twice a day for five months. I don't know if I could have talked to them about how I didn't feel worthy of existence, but they were willing to help me without question and I was willing to accept their help so that I could do the work of getting better.

The washroom situation ended up being easy to deal with. I just left the unit and used the main floor wheelchair accessible washroom.

YOU DON'T UNDERSTAND

I RETURNED TO HALIFAX to resume life with Miles after putting on twenty-eight pounds. By the end of my time at the eating disorder clinic, I still didn't love eating, but I was reconciled with the fact that I needed to eat and I deserved to eat. I was committed to having three meals and a snack every day.

I took a one-year contract as the supportive work activity program coordinator with a community organization, the Independent Living Resource Centre. I found volunteer jobs for people with disabilities and gave them whatever support they needed to make it work, be it teaching them a computer program or going with them to where they were volunteering. I was still learning to accept myself and my disability. I thought throwing myself into an environment with other people with disabilities rather than avoiding them was a good thing. In 2006, just over half of Canadians with moderate disabilities who wanted to work were able to find a job, compared to three-quarters of non-disabled people. Employment equity measures were being enacted by organizations in an effort to be progressive. I wasn't above using my disabled status to get a job — the contract I got was specifically for a person with a disability.

Working at the Centre introduced me to blind culture. My officemate, Holly, had lost her vision in her early teens. During my first week, Holly held up a sheet of paper she wanted to scan.

The computer would then read it to her using text-to-speech software.

"What side of the page has writing on it?" she asked unabashedly.

Holly accepted her blindness. She had gone to university in Ottawa, a fourteen-hour drive from Halifax. Upon her return, she moved in with her quadriplegic boyfriend. When her guide dog, Willow, retired, she chose not to get another — she didn't want to be burdened by needing to take a dog to pee. She was confident in her abilities. I wanted to be as strong as she was.

Two other blind women worked at the Centre: Julianne and Cathy. Julianne had been born with vision problems. Cathy had lost her sight due to mismanagement of her diabetes. She would eat french fries and candy without taking adequate insulin to counteract her carbohydrate intake. It must have been hard for Cathy to accept that her own actions had led to her blindness. I never had the courage to ask. How did my eating disorder contribute to the advancement of my multiple sclerosis? I have read studies about the depletion of fatty acids and how it may contribute to the demyelination of neurons.

After my year at the Centre, I volunteered with the Nova Scotia League for Equal Opportunities, an organization comprised of disability groups from across the province. When two staff members left for other jobs I was hired as their provincial coordinator, responsible for seven advocacy groups across Nova Scotia.

One day a woman in a wheelchair who was a member of NSLEO called the office. We had never met. She told me about the discrimination she had encountered in her community.

"It must be hard to face so many challenges," I said.

The woman agreed.

"Have you talked to the building owner about the situation?"

"Well, no, but providing access is the law," she said. "He should just have to do it."

"Yes, but sometimes people need a reminder."

"You don't understand how hard it is to be in a wheelchair."

"Actually, I do know what it's like to be in a wheelchair, but I don't think that excuses me from personal responsibility."

I knew I would get my knuckles rapped the next day for being insensitive to one of the clients. I had heard the speech before. Rather than try to justify my actions, I quit.

BLANK CROSSWORD

Every year, my stepdad would start growing a beard when the geese migrated south and shave it off when he spotted the first crow in spring. Early in his marriage to my mother, Jim drove heavy equipment to push down trees in northern Alberta, to clear a path for roadways. The work could only be done in the winter because the soil in that area was muskeg and if the ground wasn't frozen the heavy equipment would sink. Jim used to call on a mobile radio-telephone that only allowed one-way conversation. At the age of eight, I wasn't good at waiting for the click that signalled it was my turn to speak. From his end, the conversation went something like this:

"What did you do today?"

"... that I rode was grey."

"How was school?"

"...in the spelling exam."

Jim played cribbage while he was away, and when he returned we played together. After Jim dealt, we discussed what cards I should throw out.

"I would keep the seven and eight and the five and a face card," he said.

"But if I keep the four, I could get a longer run."

"Yeah, but you probably won't get the card you're hoping for."

It didn't matter that it would help his hand if I kept something else. Winning wasn't important to him. It was important that I was learning the game.

Eventually Jim chose to stay home because his trips to northern Alberta disrupted family life. When he stopped working up north, Mom became the primary breadwinner. This was rare in the 1980s. At the time, women earned more than men in less than 20 percent of Canadian dual-income households. Mom was careful to remind Jim of how much his being at home meant to the family.

Jim started farming grain full-time. The high input cost and instability due to weather and global grain prices meant a return was not guaranteed. He began to raise cows and hogs to supplement the allowance Mom gave him. It made him feel more in control.

When Jim's multiple sclerosis affected his ability to work on the farm, he started to work smarter. He fed and watered the livestock in the morning, rested in the afternoon and returned to the farm in the evening. He no longer raised pigs. He switched to sheep and goats because he found their smaller size more manageable.

As his multiple sclerosis worsened, I wondered if raising chickens would be more viable.

When I was twenty-five, in October 2003, Jim passed away unexpectedly.

The summer after his death, Miles and I took Mom to a cabin in rural Nova Scotia. The cabin had a deck on the front with two big Adirondack chairs and a red hummingbird feeder. Twenty metres in front of the cabin, Nova Scotia's Mersey River imbued the air with freshness.

Miles and I returned from a jaunt along the boardwalk and found Mom in one of the chairs with her legs curled under her. She had a pencil in one hand and a crossword puzzle in the other. She feigned doing the weekend puzzle but the blank answer sheet and her red eyes suggested she had been crying. I didn't know what to do. I wanted to console her but wasn't confident I could.

"Wanna go inside?" I asked.

We settled at the kitchen table. I thought about saying it was good he had died of a heart attack before his multiple sclerosis further robbed him of the ability to do the things that brought him purpose. He would have been lost without farming. He took great pride in his livestock, developing personal relationships with the animals. He once named a baby goat "Sprite" after nursing it from a Sprite bottle. He was used to being active. Having his body betray him due to multiple sclerosis was devastating, but he didn't complain. He knew it was his challenge to deal with.

My acceptance of Jim's death didn't provide my mother with any solace. She still had to crawl into an empty bed every night.

I mumbled, "I know you loved him."

She replied, "I did."

FORKING

FOR THREE YEARS MILES and I regularly visited a restaurant on the second floor of a downtown Halifax mall. It was only a few minutes from our apartment and never overly crowded. They made a good martini. Miles ordered two olives; I couldn't stand olives.

I chose carefully. I didn't want Miles to have to cut my food into smaller pieces. He would do so without question, but I didn't want to depend on him.

I avoided spaghetti and linguine because they needed to be cut. Cheese tortellini was perfect.

"How thick is the soup?" I asked the waiter.

"It's soup," he replied.

"I know, but is it brothy or thicker?"

Before I ordered, I needed to know if it was possible to get the liquid from the bowl to my mouth with a standard spoon. I routinely lost the contents of a mouthful before it actually got to my mouth. I thought I had it solved when I bent a spoon at home to face myself, forming the letter L. That way I didn't have to turn my wrist with the spoon. It didn't fit neatly into the plastic silverware divider but it helped. Food I could spear with a fork was easy to eat. Once speared, the tines of the fork held the mouthful in place, even when my hands shook.

Two years after the restaurant experience I sat at my dining room table eating bananas and yogurt for breakfast. The banana was easy to spear — the challenge was getting it to my mouth. Using a full fist, I speared a piece with a fork held in my left hand, which had more grip than the right, and then changed my grasp to the right hand. To move it to my mouth I wanted my thumb on top of the fork, my index finger and middle finger grasping the fork from the bottom of the handle. I swung the speared banana to the level of my mouth. I opened my mouth wide. I contracted my arm muscles to bring the fork closer to my gaping mouth.

I cringed as wet banana hit my right cheek.

Damn it.

I fumbled for a napkin to wipe the yogurt off my face.

I reset and tried again. I caught the left corner of my lip with yogurt-covered banana but was able to deflect it into the gaping hole.

I wiped the corner of my mouth. I used the same napkin as before, careful to avoid the first wet spot.

One piece down, twelve to go.

COUNT TO TEN

HER PARTNER WRAPPED HIS arms around her extended belly as they gazed out on the Halifax harbour. She must have been seven or eight months pregnant. Miles and I passed them on the boardwalk but there were no caresses, no gentle words between us.

We were fighting constantly. That morning started with Miles criticizing what I was wearing.

"I wish you wouldn't wear that," he said. Miles hated my hoodies.

"What's wrong with it?"

"It makes you look juvenile."

"It's warm. Do you want me to be cold?"

"I just wish you'd stop wearing those."

There was a hamper for the Boys and Girls Club in the basement of our apartment building. All my hoodies went there. I was willing to discard the real me to be what I thought Miles wanted in a partner. He deserved to have a woman who made him happy — I was determined to become that woman.

I never let myself throw anything at Miles, not even soft things like socks or a pillow. I was taught not to throw in anger. In Alberta, I would have punched the garage door until my knuckles bled. In Halifax, I tried to slam the bedroom door. I wanted it to slam in Miles's face as I shouted, "I can't stand it!" Instead of a satisfying slam, the door waffled on its hinges.

While I was home for the Christmas holidays, I asked my mother, a registered counsellor, for some advice. I wanted Miles to understand we had to be patient for our relationship to work. He expected me to respond as quickly as the computer programs he worked with all day. If I didn't answer him quickly enough, he'd let out a sigh and start doing something else. Miles and I had been attending couples counselling, but things weren't progressing as I hoped.

"How do I make sure I don't blow up and say something I don't mean?" I asked my mom.

"I know it's cliché but you could count to ten."

"I think I ought to count to a hundred."

I started using Mom's trick when I got back to Halifax. Miles and I continued with counselling.

"How do you think things are going?" I asked. Counselling was expensive. I wanted to ensure he was committed to fixing our relationship.

"I think the therapist is really understanding," said Miles.

"I agree, but are you comfortable talking with her?"

"I tell her what I think she wants to hear."

"What you think she wants to hear? So, not the truth? How is she going to help?"

He didn't have an answer.

AROUND MY TWENTY-EIGHTH BIRTHDAY, the sphincter on my urethra stopped following my commands. I would sit down to pee but nothing would come. I put my hand in warm water as they do in freshmen-dorm-initiation movies. I tried Advil, which I thought, as a muscle relaxant, should relax my bladder muscles enough to let me pee. I tried self-catheterization, which involves sticking a thin tube inside the urethra. It slides past the opening of the sphincter and the pee goes down the tube like a straw draining a pot of chicken broth. But my motor coordination wasn't what it should have been and I couldn't always find the opening to stick the tube in.

"Miles?" I asked, "I have to pee but I can't find the hole to my urethra. Will you help?' I could find my vagina easily enough but that didn't do me any good.

Miles was hesitant. "You want me to do what?"

Catheterizing me changed the way Miles saw me. I was no longer his girlfriend — I was someone he nursed.

I started to wear Depends — a girlfriend in diapers is not sexy.

The diaper couldn't hold all the urine I produced during a day at work. The diaper filled up, the urine seeped out, soaked through my pants and dripped on the floor. At the end of the day I was sitting in a diaper overflowing with stale urine. There are only so many days you can tell the janitor you spilled apple juice.

I didn't want a permanent catheter: a tube running out of my urethra into a bag collecting urine hanging off the side of the bed or strapped to my ankle. How would any guy find a vagina with a tube next to it alluring? At least with the diapers, there was hope of sex.

I met with a urologist. He told me about suprapubic catheters which went directly into the bladder, a couple of inches beneath the belly button. No tube near the vagina.

After the operation, a simple day surgery, I thought Miles would want me again.

I lay next to him in bed and asked, "Wanna get it on?"

"I'm tired."

"But I haven't peed myself."

Miles turned on his reading lamp and picked up a book.

LITTER BOX

MILES WENT TO THE office for the afternoon. He had a bunch of work to catch up on. He wouldn't be home until supper — five or six hours away.

We had just moved into my new condo, where we could have a cat, so we adopted one from the SPCA. I was enamoured by anything to do with that persistent meower — even the litter box.

After Miles had gone, I gathered the pooper-scooper and plastic bag and set off to clean the litter box. I pulled the box to an area where I had enough room to park. My wheelchair was lightweight so I had the strength to push it myself. The downside was that the design of the frame made it tippy.

I took the lid off the litter box.

I should have parked so that I had to reach sideways to scoop out the poo — but I didn't.

I should have ordered extra wheels on the front of my chair to make it more secure — but I didn't.

I reached forward — a little too far.

Damn.

I could feel the chair falling forward. My hands, already out in front of me, stopped my head from hitting the litter.

Fuck.

The litter, about six inches from my face, smelled chalky. Its grit cut into my hands. I had already scooped most of the poop out, so at least my nose wasn't millimetres from a piece of cat shit.

What were my options? Miles wouldn't be back for at least another three hours. My arms were beginning to shake from the weight they were holding. Perspiration was forming on the back of my neck. My glasses were steaming up from my heavy breathing. Five minutes passed.

I couldn't right the chair.

"Help! Help!"

My cry echoed through the empty condo. I hoped it would reverberate into the hallway.

The front door of the condo opened a crack. The building super stuck his head in tentatively. I knew Paul from the chats we had while I waited outside for Access-A-Bus, the door-to-door accessible bus service. Each time we spoke, Paul recounted how he had fallen six storeys in an industrial painting accident. He should have been killed or at least paralyzed, but he wasn't. He had metal rods holding his ankles together and was always in a significant amount of pain. Paul felt we had a kinship because he also had a disability.

To him, I was Jenny. I never corrected him by telling him I went by Jen.

"Jenny?" he asked in his thick Acadian accent.

"Oh my God, Paul. Help me."

Paul followed the sound of my voice.

"My God, Jenny. Are you okay?"

Paul was strong enough to right the chair with me in it.

The half-changed litter box was waiting for Miles to finish when he returned.

TAKING POSSESSION

RATHER THAN RELY ON Miles for drives, I started depending on Access-A-Bus. I met a bus driver named Charles. He was cute. He was always in a good mood and joked a lot with the passengers.

"Flash me your bus pass — or just flash me."

As far as I know, no one took him up on his offer, but one day I lifted my shirt for him. As promised, I rode free that day.

His blue Access-A-Bus sweater was pushed up above his elbows as he passed me the change from my bus fare, and I noticed he had a tattoo sleeve on his left arm. It was a turn-on. I saw an invitation to ask him about tattoo parlours and how to go about getting body art.

After a decade of contemplating getting a tattoo, I finally made the decision to actually do it. I had tried to control my body by not eating. Now that I was eating, I needed another way of exerting control. A tattoo seemed like a healthy way to take possession of my body.

I decided on a poppy for my design. Poppies had decorated the Ukrainian dance costumes I wore when I was a teenager. It was the perfect flower for my tattoo, but I didn't know where to put it. I knew I didn't want artwork on my forehead like the tattoo artist and owner of The Laughing Dragon on Dutch Village Road. Because I was in a wheelchair, the artist refused to put any tattoos on my lower body.

"Without walking, I don't think you'd have enough blood return for the tattoo to heal properly. The upper arm is always a good area to put a tattoo and it won't be too painful."

I agreed.

Coordinating the trip to the tattoo artist's studio was tricky. Miles said he could take me there but wouldn't wait the hour and a half it would take to emblazon the flower on my arm.

I asked bus driver Charles to pick me up at the end of my appointment, and he agreed to. As it happened, Charles was early and Miles dragged his heels so they collided at the tattoo studio, which was thrilling for me — I was signalling to Miles I could find another man.

Charles lifted me with such care into his Volkswagen Jetta. It was cool to be in a car that wasn't Miles's red four-by-four.

Once it healed, I could decipher the lines of the tattoo. It was a rose — not a poppy. I was angry, but what could I do? The lines were in black ink and no tattoo artist could colour over them.

Women often admired my tattoo. "I love roses, too."

I would reply, "I hate roses."

Five years earlier, Miles had a dozen red roses delivered to my workplace in celebration of my first birthday with him. I was crushed. Not only was I allergic to roses, for a month I had hinted at how much I despised them. Miles hadn't listened.

OTHER MEN

ONCE, IN THE INITIAL months of our relationship, coated by a fine sheen of perspiration, Miles and I lay on a green sheet covering his queen-size bed. It was Saturday, mid-afternoon. The sun was streaming into our bedroom. I was still in post-orgasmic glee.

"Miles, will you marry me?"

"No."

I felt illegitimate, like the woman my father cheated on my mother with but would not marry.

"Why not? Aren't you happy with me?"

"I don't believe in marriage. Anyhow, we should have talked about marriage before you moved in if that's where you thought this was heading."

Five years later, I was still in love with Miles, but I needed to be touched. We were sitting next to some potted junipers at a downtown restaurant on Argyle Street, in the heart of Halifax. We had just ordered brunch.

"Miles, would you mind if I slept with another guy?" There, I spat it out. I had practised in my mind for hours. "We aren't doing much of anything and I still want sex."

Miles replied, "Go ahead."

The idea of an open relationship conflicted with my Christian upbringing. I was raised to think the only man you should sleep with is the man you plan to marry.

"If you're not happy, Miles, why don't you leave?" I asked.

"How would it look if I left a disabled woman?"

I wasn't hopeful I would find another partner. Should I advertise on Kijiji or Plenty of Fish? What would my ad look like? *Disabled woman seeks sexual partner. No commitment required.*

Only a few weeks after the open relationship discussion, as I was wheeling towards the bus, driver Charles asked me what my plans were for the weekend. I told him that my boyfriend was away on business and while the cat was away his mouse would play. I flirted with all the bus drivers. I thought their jobs were pretty tedious and they deserved some distraction.

Charles replied, "If you want to play, I'm free."

Charles and I set up a date.

It was that simple. One little suggestion and I had a partner. Now I had to figure out how to execute the plan. I loved Miles enough not to defile his bed with my rendezvous. Charles and I "slept" in the spare bedroom.

I had to tell Charles about the catheter before we had sex. I had to admit that I did not have dominion over my eager body.

"Is there anything I have to watch out for?" Charles asked.

"I don't think so. I haven't had sex with anyone since I had it put in."

"So this will be the test drive."

"I guess." I couldn't believe how nonchalant he was.

"Sex is never perfect. We all have our quirks. I've never dealt with yours before but I'm sure we'll be fine," said Charles.

That was it? It was a big deal to Miles.

Charles was rough but the catheter was fine. There was a little blood in my urine afterward from the end of the catheter scraping against the wall of my bladder but it still worked. The bus driver's attitude helped me to become more accepting of my body and who I was. I gained confidence in my ability to satisfy my desires and those of my partner.

A month later, The Rolling Stones played in Halifax. Though I was scheduled to go to the concert with Miles, Charles asked me to go with him and I accepted. He was wearing his big yellow raincoat as it had been pouring all day. Neither of us had brought any food so he bought pizza from the concession. He fed it to me, without complaint, shaking the water from his hands like a kitten.

Some people in the disability section recognized Charles from the bus and called "Hey, Charles." He addressed them by name with a hearty "Hello," but stayed next to me. We were at the show as a couple. After a dozen years on the path of multiple sclerosis, it was finally okay to sit in the "crips" section, to admit the condition I had tried to deny. Charles's acceptance of my disability was exactly what I needed.

Charles had just broken up with his wife and wasn't comfortable staying in their marital home. This worked for me. Miles and I were only together so there was someone around to pick me up if I fell. Since Charles needed a place to live, I asked Miles to move. He didn't seem to like that I had found someone who made me happy, but he recognized that I owned the condo and that he had agreed to let me see other men.

Charles moved in on the day Miles moved out.

MY FIRST ASSISTANT

Anne Sinclair, the professor of the first-year architecture class, apologized, "We can find another room. I didn't realize that this one isn't fully accessible."

I reassured her, "No this room is perfect. It demonstrates what architects need to think about when designing a space for all users."

A week later, I delivered a lecture from the top of the ramp.

"The auditorium looks like it will be great for people with disabilities, the ramp deposits wheelchair users into two spots, each at the end of a row in the middle of the audience. This is a refreshing change from the usual designations at the very back or the very front of the room. But, from those two spots there are stairs to the front, where presentations are delivered. What the designer is saying is that wheelchair users are invited to come listen to the speakers the school of architecture and planning has brought in. However, a wheelchair user cannot actually be one of the presenters."

At the end of my talk, Jill Grant, the director of the School of Planning asked, "Have you ever thought about becoming a student here? You have some great insights."

A few months later I was accepted into the School of Planning at Dalhousie University, but I wouldn't be successful on my own — I needed help. I couldn't reliably drive my power wheelchair to class. I couldn't feed myself. So I hired Michelle.

Michelle was a certified teacher. She had been teaching in Korea but had missed the application deadline for a position with Halifax Regional School Board. She had long dark hair and was at home in an educational setting. I worked with my assistants so much and so closely that we often became friends. Michelle had been with her partner for a few weeks and wasn't sure when she should start sleeping with him. We talked about things that made us feel insecure about our relationships, and she made me feel better about living with Charles, which I had found was much different than living with Miles.

In order to do the schoolwork, Michelle read aloud to me, and I wrote by dictation. We completed exams the same way. In one case, the professor ushered us outside his classroom to do a quiz. If we had stayed, Michelle's voice ringing through the classroom would have been disruptive.

Michelle sat on the gleaming linoleum. I parked next to her. In response to a question she read aloud, I spouted off an answer. Michelle raised an eyebrow. She had read most of the cases the exam covered aloud to me so she was familiar with the content.

"Are you sure?" she asked.

I wasn't sure. Her eyebrow raise made me stop and reconsider my answer. It was an open book exam so I consulted the actual case, rather than rely on memory. I got Michelle to read the case's conclusion and answered again. This time, Michelle recorded my response.

A few weeks later I got the exam results — I received the top mark in the class.

THERE HAD BEEN A storm overnight but classes went forward with their regular schedule. I made it a policy not to miss class. I was sure that if I did, the prof would choose that class in which to unlock the secret to the universe. I had to be there just in case. The fresh snow covered my ankles, it was soft and clean but too dense for my chair to push aside. I had sent Michelle into the building to see if she could find a shovel. She found the Maggie, the custodian. As Maggie shovelled the snow from the ramp, she muttered

"The university hires other people to do things like this you know, but Jen, I'll make sure you get to class."

I nominated Maggie for a Dalhousie award for outstanding service. She demonstrated how I needed a community behind me in order to succeed. She was one of the four recipients that year.

YOU'RE A NURSE,
AREN'T YOU?

THOUGH I'D BEGUN TO use a power wheelchair that fall, I still used my manual wheelchair on flights. It was common for my chair to be handled roughly, especially at Christmas when luggage holds are fuller than usual. There was less chance the airline would damage my manual chair.

Having spent Christmas with my family in Alberta I was flying back to Halifax. The flight from Edmonton to Toronto was uneventful. Once we landed, the crew announced that the flight from Toronto to Halifax would be delayed until the following morning. A storm in Halifax made landing impossible.

The flight attendant was chipper: "If you don't go to a hotel, we encourage you to pull up a foam pad and sleep in the waiting room."

I panicked. What would I do? I couldn't transfer out of my chair independently. Shit. Deep breath. The flight attendants and captain went off to their hotels. Even the customer service personnel went home.

I went to the washroom. I considered asking for help. It would be simple. All someone needed to do was empty my leg bag into a cup, the contents of which could then be poured into the toilet. I had a cup in my carry-on, but I wanted to appear competent. Competent women didn't ask for help. But my leg bag was almost full. I lacked the dexterity to remove the cap from the spout and pull the blue lever forward to empty it. If it wasn't emptied, the urine would fill the bag, then my bladder, and the sphincter on my bladder would release. I would pee like normal but I wouldn't be near a toilet — my skirt would be soaked.

To travel on the plane, I had to transfer from my wheelchair to a Washington chair, no wider than a beverage cart, to be wheeled down the aisle. My regular chair was put in the luggage hold. This transfer happened on the ramp outside the plane. I would be wheeled to my row in the plane, then lifted from the Washington chair to an airplane seat. The airline personnel would notice if I were dripping urine when one of them grabbed me under the knees and the other under my armpits. How could I sit my urine-soaked derrière on the airplane seat? What about the person who would use that seat on the next flight?

I had to empty my leg bag.

Lester B. Pearson Airport was big enough to warrant a medical office. I had to find it. The medical staff should help me without judgment. I asked a security guard to push me there.

It was midnight. The airport hallways were quiet, though still brightly lit. The sign on the medical office door stated it would reopen at 7:00 a.m.

I parked outside the office and waited.

At three in the morning my leg bag became full and I peed myself.

My flight boarded at quarter to eight that morning. I would have forty-five minutes from the opening of the medical office to my boarding time. I could do this.

Jangling keys woke me at seven. The nurse had arrived. I waited for him to usher me in.

A few minutes later, I wheeled in, shutting the door. It was a well-stocked room smelling of hospital, with an examination table.

"Sorry, my plane's boarding in a few minutes so we need to do this quickly. I had an accident — I peed myself. Can you help me take off this soiled skirt? We could fashion a new wrap-around skirt with this blanket from the flight."

"I don't deal with that kind of thing. I treat broken ankles and chest pain."

"You're a nurse, aren't you?" I assumed people went into nursing because they wanted to help.

He replied, "Yes. An R.N."

"Just because you don't usually help with things like leg bags and skirt changes doesn't mean you *can't* help."

He looked skeptical.

I tried again, "You were hired by the airport to help passengers. I'm a passenger. I told you how you can help me."

We emptied the leg bag and took off the dirty skirt. Using a couple of safety pins, we fashioned a makeshift skirt.

That was the last time I flew without a diaper.

ROOMMATES

CHARLES AND I DIDN'T last. We were two different people in two different places in our lives, and it just didn't work. I had a lot of baggage from my relationship with Miles. Charles had a lot to work through after his marriage ended. When he moved out I had to hire an assistant who could turn me at night when the position I was sleeping in became uncomfortable. Instead of paying someone directly, I offered a room in my condo with the condition my roommate would be home five nights out of seven to put me to bed and sleep with a baby monitor in case I called and needed to be turned.

I wanted a roommate with common sense and compassion, not formal caregiver training. I found my first roommate through an ad on Kijiji. The young woman, Carol, had auditioned for a job as a barmaid at Alexander Keith's Historic Brewery and was waiting to hear back, so she was glad to have a place to live rent-free.

One evening Carol went to hang out with friends around eight. "See you at ten," I called as the door slammed shut.

Ten passed.

Eleven passed.

Midnight passed.

At one, I called Miles out of desperation. He lived less than a block away. He could put me into bed.

My roommate arrived as Miles was taking off his shoes. She reeked of alcohol.

She told me, "Don't worry. I can put you into bed."

Miles looked to me for a response.

I said, "I don't think so."

That was strike one, and it was a big strike. Two other screw-ups and she would be looking for another place to live. She was gone by the end of the month.

I placed an ad on the Dalhousie Student Career website to find Jen-sitters, people to stay overnight on the two nights a week my roommate didn't need to be at home. Mom was visiting and participated in the interviews for Jen-sitters.

Misha walked into the condo wearing a black baseball cap. Mom, a former school principal, was used to standing at the main door of the school and hollering at any student who dared cross the threshold with anything but a toque on their head. It was northern Alberta — toques were allowed. In Mom's opinion, the fact that Misha did not take off his hat eliminated him as a candidate for employment. I saw the hat as a shield that Misha wore to fend off attacking glances. He was alone in a foreign country. I thought he needed a friend. I overruled Mom and hired Misha.

He explained how he had received his medical training in the Soviet Union. In the late 1980s, the USSR gave scholarships to medical students from developing nations as a way of building goodwill. During his first shift as a Jen-sitter, Misha told me he had given up medicine in South Asia to accompany his wife to Victoria, British Columbia, where she was pursuing her PhD in computer science.

One day, Misha walked in on his wife having sex with a fellow student. He was crushed. He had given up everything for her. He had left his brother and sister, his aging mother, the country he loved and the profession he excelled at. He could not even return to practise medicine as his government considered that he had abandoned his post as a physician. Misha didn't want to chance running into his adulterous wife, so he moved across Canada to pursue a degree in health informatics at Dalhousie.

I wanted to show Misha his life could have purpose even if he wasn't a practising doctor. He could use his skills and compassion in other ways. Misha didn't have a work permit at the time. Rather than pay him, I sent money to his sister, who was an education professor in his home country. Her students were often sent to remote rural areas where the government had built schools but hadn't bothered to supply the libraries. She used the money I sent to buy books.

Misha worked as a Jen-sitter for six months before I asked him to be my roommate. Misha had a better-than-you attitude that annoyed me but he could take my pulse — which I found sexy. Living in my condo would be perfect for Misha. He wouldn't have to stay in residence, so it would save him money, something he didn't have much of.

Misha was my moral compass. He explained that while Christians can ask for forgiveness and have their sins taken away, Buddhists carry their past actions with them. If I faced a moral decision, he told me to choose my actions wisely because I would live with the consequences my whole life.

At that time, I felt that my judgment was compromised. I was desperately looking for sexual gratification. I wanted to feel desired — I needed to shake off the ghost of Miles's sexual indifference. I wasn't leading the respectable life of a well-raised Christian girl. If my grandmother knew what I was up to, she would have been horrified. I was talking dirty on Plenty of Fish. I routinely had phone sex. I performed a blowjob in the parkade of my condominium on a married man. He had been wearing the same track pants he wore when he coached his sons' hockey team. Misha steered me onto a different path.

HE USED TO LIFT me from my chair into bed, cradling me with both arms. One night, my catheter must have been blocked because as soon as he picked me up and turned to put me onto the bed, my bladder emptied. I peed on his black house shoes. Neither of us spoke.

Then he laughed. "I was trained as a doctor," he said. "I've seen worse."

I was mortified. He hadn't seen worse from me.

I bought Misha a pair of flip-flops as compensation. I may not have been able to control my body but I could control my response. The flip-flops were washable.

When Misha left for a job in Newfoundland, I had to look for a new roommate. Although a wiser person may have learned her lesson, I advertised on Kijiji a second time.

I hired a single mother with a three-year-old son. She was a university student. I thought a single mom would be an ideal roommate. A mother would need to be home for her child, therefore would be home to help me. Adding an extra baby monitor would be simple. I thought this would allow me to witness a child grow and develop, since I knew I was unlikely to have children of my own.

When my sister had children I was relieved from any responsibility to make sure my parents had grandkids. But when I saw a family with young children, I longed for that to be my reality. The baby, the excitement. I wanted to see the world as a child sees it, unblemished and new. I am capable of having children. I am still able to ovulate, but I take birth control pills continuously so I don't get my period. It would be awkward to ask my assistants or homecare workers to change a tampon. I didn't have a committed partner, but there are sperm banks and men who would be happy to have sex without a condom, but I couldn't hold an infant to my breast. I couldn't run after a toddler. I couldn't raise a child.

I didn't anticipate how I would feel when I couldn't intervene in my roommate's parenting. Her son's health was never at risk, but I disagreed with her choices. She often gave her son a Halloween treat-sized bag of Doritos for breakfast, and though she normally cooked supper for her son, I once saw her feed him a tablespoon of peanut butter instead of a meal. When he brought a banana and a butcher knife to me in bed one morning, asking me to cut the fruit open for him, I questioned the wisdom of the arrangement. When he started playing with lighters, I knew it wasn't viable. His mother assured me that the lighter did not contain any lighter fluid so it was harmless, but I couldn't stop imagining what would happen if he got his hands on a working lighter one day.

She only stayed one semester. After four months, she was accepted for subsidized housing and moved over Christmas break.

However iffy my relationships with my roommates may have been, the people I met because of those roommates were amazing. Ali tutored the single mum. The tutor, a soccer player and PhD student in computer science, and I became friends.

I have my old manual chair in my condo just in case I should ever need it. Ali decided to take the manual chair for a spin. He was racing me in my power chair. I live near both the Saint Mary's and Dalhousie university campuses, so it was common to find a group of students drinking on their front porch. They were cheering Ali along. He was travelling fast in the manual chair. Then he hit a rock. The wheelchair began to fall forward. The gasp from the crowd was audible.

Then Ali suddenly put his feet under him and rose out of the chair. It was a modern-day miracle. The crowd fell silent, and Ali and I fled the scene, not wanting to face accusations of impersonating the disabled.

PAYING THE BILLS

"Your father asked me what would happen if we stopped putting money in your bank account."

"What would happen? The sky would fall."

I wouldn't be able to pay for my condo. I wouldn't be able to pay my assistants. I would have to go to the food bank.

For my mother it was a passing comment, but for me thoughts of institutional living invaded my dreams. My high-care needs meant I would be warehoused in a nursing home.

I've never known financial poverty, have never gone without a meal because my cupboards were bare. I pick the cheapest spaghetti sauce at the grocery store because I'm conscious of cost, not because I have to.

When I worked for NSLEO I was asked to participate in a workshop on poverty. I was part of a panel speaking about the inadequacies of Income Assistance. As I'm a disabled woman, the organizers probably assumed I'd had personal experience. Their assumptions were reasonable. In 2006, 19.9 percent of Canadians with severe disabilities reported receiving welfare benefits — 25.4 percent if the disability was categorized as very severe. At the same time, 27.5 percent of Canadian women categorized as having severe or very severe disability fell into the low-income category, while only 16.4 percent of men reported the same. The average income for women with severe or very severe disability was $16,481, compared to $24,073 for men.

I felt inadequate to talk about Income Assistance. I had book knowledge, but everyone else on the panel actually survived on Income Assistance. I didn't feel worthy of my seat.

The big topic was why men and women got the same amount of social assistance even though women had to pay for tampons and other sanitary supplies.

One woman's case worker said, "Well, men have the expense of condoms."

The woman replied, "Men choose to have sex — I don't choose to get my period."

Having a disability without having money is a different experience than having a disability while being able to pay for modified equipment and living space, and support.

I didn't have to apply to the Department of Community Services to cover the cost of the $180 gel pad I needed to prevent pressure sores, and then wait for months to get my application approved. If my occupational therapist said I needed it, I could buy it.

I am lucky enough to have a family who can provide me with enough money to maintain a great quality of life. But, I know Dad wants me to come home. He's getting older and dreams of retiring. In Alberta, there are better government support programs for people with severe disability. But my independence is in Halifax. My life is in Halifax. In one way, I am dependent in Halifax, but it is a dependence I have chosen.

THE ECOLOGY
ACTION CENTRE

AFTER COMPLETING MY MASTER'S degree in land-use planning, I was hired onto the transportation team at the Ecology Action Centre, Nova Scotia's premier environmental organization. Again, I was accompanied by an assistant. Nova Scotia didn't have a program to pay for this support, so I paid my assistant out of my salary. I would be in charge of motorized transportation issues, including rail, transit and automobile. This meant I set up a petition against the widening of a major artery, fought against the conversion of Halifax's rail cut to automotive use, partnered with Car Share Halifax and developed an integrated mobility plan for the municipality.

I was one of the two EAC employees who routinely used an automobile to get to work rather than a more sustainable method. I couldn't depend on the Access-a-bus service to deliver me to work every day. Taking the regular bus was possible but I felt that I took too long to board. It was slow to drive my chair onto the ramp and turn around. Having the driver attach my chair to the floor ate into the schedule.

The single parking spot at the Ecology Action Centre led onto a ramp that terminated on the back patio near the kitchen door. Along the back ramp was a trellis of willow branches. The leaves fluttered in front of my forehead unless the gardening crew had trimmed it. If they hadn't then the overhanging branches slapped me in the face. Finally, my assistant packed gardening shears. "We will deal with the problem ourselves," she quipped.

The ramp switched back from the trellis of willows to be adjacent to the garden. The fragrance of sweet raspberries greeted me in late July. Treading farther along, we passed the basil growing at the corner, a spot where the gardening team hoped that it would catch both the morning and the afternoon sunlight. Right before the door was a cherry tomato plant. I monitored the progress of a single tomato, trying to figure out how to coerce my assistant to pluck it from the vine at the perfect stage of orange. One day my tomato was gone.

Because of my Slavic heritage, my family follows both the old and the new calendar, celebrating Ukrainian Christmas on January 7. Having spent the last couple of weeks with family, I wanted to start the new year with a gathering of friends and workplace associates. I hosted a Ukrainian Christmas party following the traditions I learned in childhood. I asked my EAC colleague Jamie to provide live music for the potluck-style celebration. He played a mean violin in addition to being a champion for Nova Scotia forests. I remember his tawny beard on the chin piece and his lively dip and sway. I was worried about the neighbours complaining as he rocked the living room all evening.

TAKING RISKS

LIZ, TWENTY-THREE, WHO WAS looking both for a change and to save some money, was my new roommate. Seven days after she moved in I asked her to accompany me to Montreal, where my co-worker Laena Garrison and I were attending a conference. Liz would have to dress me and wash my face and pubic area, tasks usually reserved for home care.

At Montreal's Trudeau Airport, Liz, Laena, the other transportation coordinator at the EAC, and I ordered an accessible taxi. The driver was a young Algerian man. I asked, "What's the best Algerian restaurant in Montreal?"

He looked at us in the rear-view mirror, evaluating our trustworthiness. Three youngish women, one of whom was in a wheelchair. How dangerous could we be?

"I can take you there tomorrow night. I'm not working but I have a van."

Liz and I looked at each other. "Why not?"

Neither of us realized that our driver would be picking us up in his own minivan, which wasn't wheelchair accessible. Neither had we considered the danger of going with a strange man in a strange city.

The next day, the cab driver arrived at our downtown hotel. He thought he could just pick me and my chair up and put me into his minivan. He could, I'm small (even with the chair I was only 130

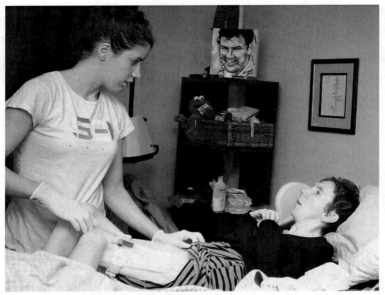

Homecare worker Jillian emptying Jen's leg bag, spring 2015.
(photo courtesy of Snickerdoodle Photography)

pounds) but he didn't account for the fact that wheelchair accessible vans have lowered floors. It's a good thing I'm short — my head was only millimetres from the doorframe. Liz covered my face with her scarf so my nose wouldn't scrape on the door moulding.

The driver seemed like a nice guy. On the way to the restaurant he told us that he bought his four-year-old daughter a snowsuit for her upcoming birthday. I was happy to imagine him playing in the snow with her.

The cab driver went into the restaurant, leaving Liz and me in the van. He said he was going to talk to the owner. We assumed he was telling the owner it was fine that we weren't Algerian. He took us into the restaurant, said he'd be back later and was gone.

My adventure in Montreal provided much needed relief from my calculated existence. Usually, I plan who is going to be with me every moment of every day. I get up at the same time every day. I go to bed at the same time every evening. I have scheduled bowel movements. I have scheduled times to wash my hair. I shave under my arms with the same homecare worker every second week. Before I go to restaurants, I call to evaluate how accessible they really are. I don't make spur-of-the moment decisions. Being in the cab driver's non-accessible van made me remember the thrill of spontaneity. The restaurant was excellent, and true to his word, the driver returned as we were finishing our dessert.

WHEN HE ARRIVED FOR his interview, Mike had three days' worth of stubble, two diamond studs and a blue bandana hanging out of his back pocket. I asked if he had read the job description.

Mike played football and taught gymnastics. I was sure he was too cool for me, but was comfortable doing personal care. He wasn't so comfortable with the fact that I was the boss. He wanted me to have more fun.

The first thing he encouraged me to do was to make my bucket list, things I wanted to do before I died. I wanted to investigate a therapeutic option for treating my multiple sclerosis. I felt guilty for not following multiple sclerosis research. I didn't go to any support groups. I thought I should be doing more. I had received an email from one of the mailing lists I subscribed to with a link to a video about conductive education (CE). The video showed how conductive ed was helping kids with cerebral palsy to walk.

Founded on the work of Hungarian physical therapist András Pető, conductive ed adheres to the principle that clients must be active participants in their treatment. Working with the individual as a whole and giving credence to the brain's plasticity, conductive ed reteaches the body and mind the skills and movements the human body was constructed for. Conductive ed never packaged itself as a miracle cure, so I was willing to look into it. Mike accompanied me to my first appointment.

At the first session, I met conductive educators Beth and Rachel. They were young and eager. They began the session by telling me I would stand by the end of the day. I was incredulous.

After assessing my strength and movement, they put knee braces, constructed out of rulers in a fabric case, onto my legs. The braces would keep my knees from buckling. With Rachel behind me and Beth at my side, they levered me into a standing position. I could feel my weight through my heels and toes. I didn't stand for long, maybe five seconds, but they were five miraculous seconds.

NEAR THE TOP OF my bucket list was swimming in the Atlantic. Coming from Alberta, I had never swum in an ocean. I told Mike I wanted to cross it off my list. He said, "Easy."

Right. Swimming in the Atlantic without the use of my arms and legs — that's easy.

A swimming opportunity arose with the EAC Fun Day, held in August on what turned out to be a foggy day at Rainbow Haven Beach. The beach's whiteboard recorded the ocean's temperature at fourteen degrees Celsius. It was so cold the only people on the beach were from the EAC. Two of my colleagues who had planned to go swimming chickened out when they felt the temperature of the water. My colleague Carla lent me her wetsuit booties, "You're going to need them."

Mike held my weight while my roommate Liz, who was a life-guard, stood by just in case. The policy director of the EAC was the spotter. I considered not going in because of the water temperature, but everything was in place: Liz, Mike and the wetsuit booties. The whoosh of the crashing waves increased my excitement.

Mike carried me into the ocean. The water rose from my butt to my chest, feeling colder the farther we walked. The buoyancy and the rolling waves were unlike anything I had experienced.

After the swim, Mike gently placed me back in my manual wheelchair. "How was that?"

"Amazing," I answered. "You were so steady. Were you cold?"

He dismissed my concern about him, "Jen, it was all about you."

Liz rushed me to the change room to put on some dry clothes. "How was that?"

"I think my skirt was hanging off my butt and you could see my underwear."

Liz assured me, "I don't think anyone looked at your butt. I think everyone was watching the smile on your face."

Bryan, another assistant, waited for me in the warm van. "How was it?" he asked.

The cold water had reduced the inflammation in my spinal cord. I was able to lift my arms. I was able to hold my hand in front of my face and examine the little scars I hadn't seen for years. "Amazing. I should swim in cold water every day."

But the cold had penetrated every cell of my body. I spent the next two days in bed, shivering.

I COULD FEEL THE heat of Jamie's body emanating through his t-shirt. My right cheek was pressed against his back. His skin was moist, a function of climbing at the hottest part of the day. I was strapped into a backpack device fastened around his chest and his waist as we were about to rappel down the side of the two-storey Ecology Action Centre building.

Jamie, the forestry coordinator at the EAC, and I had become friends because he passed my office on the way to the stairs which led to his office. I always said hello because I admired his dedication to saving the land from rampant clear-cutting. I also thought he was cute.

Dedicated to his chosen sport of mountain climbing, he owned all the rope and carabiners we needed. Wayne, our colleague who worked on energy projects, helped us reach the roof through the hatch designed for accessing the solar panels. As Jamie neared the edge of the roof my exuberance grew. I never believed I would actually rappel down the side of 2705 Fern Lane. My heartbeat accelerated, my breathing became shallow. Why had we decided to do this at midday? It was hot, would Jamie's bare hands slip on the rope? Would his grey and red climbing shoes provide enough traction? His abilities were the only thing between me and the hard pavement two storeys below.

The financial director's soft, no nonsense voice cut through my daydream.

"If you ever were silly enough to rappel down the EAC," she pronounced, "we would never get insurance coverage again. I absolutely forbid any of you to try such a thing." Some days I wished my office wasn't across the hall from hers. She had obviously heard Jamie and me discussing our plan.

MEETING TOM

AN EMAIL FROM EVELYN Jones, in charge of refugee sponsorship with the Metro Immigrant Settlement Association (later known as Immigrant Services Association of Nova Scotia), called for sponsorship groups to help settle Palestinian refugees left stateless by the war in Iraq. In 2009, Rachel, one of my assistants, read the email. After a meeting with the program coordinator, Rachel, my former roommate Liz and I, along with a woman named Linda, agreed to sponsor a family. With a few friends and community volunteers, we formed Friends for Refugees (FFR).

We raised $26,000 to sponsor a husband, wife and their two kids. We had to find and furnish an apartment, ensure the kids were registered for school, find a suitable doctor, help with language acquisition and coordinate dental check-ups for the kids. The family spoke little English, so having Arabic translators was imperative.

My dealings with the family were limited. I found it difficult to communicate with non-English speakers without the use of my hands to gesticulate. The family's apartment was in an older building with four stairs to the front door. Although they were willing to meet outside the main door of their building, it was cold and public.

When I realized how tight the refugees' budget was, I wanted to give them more. I had more, why shouldn't they? But, our family was part of a larger group of related families, and we wanted to ensure they were all treated equally. I couldn't afford to give every family more support — which would ultimately come out of my parents' pockets — so I decided a more sensible approach was to work harder at fundraising.

Sam, one of FFR's volunteers, was organizing a screening of several animated shorts on peaceful conflict resolution. She held a preliminary screening in her office to find out FFR members' opinions on what films should comprise the program. She brought her friend Tom in for technical assistance. In the elevator I greeted him warmly. He grunted. He later explained he had walked to the screening in the rain. He hated the rain.

One of the films we watched was *Robes of War*, an animation by Michèle Cournoyer. Rachel said, "Do you think that portrayal of the woman in the burqa makes the film anti-Islamic?"

I said, "I think it portrays how followers of Islam feel the agony of war. Besides, that last shot was reminiscent of Michaelangelo's *Pietà*."

Tom spoke up, "That's a very Catholic symbol."

I was thrilled that Tom commented on my observation. He was cute. And if he knew the reference, he was also smart.

Sam invited Tom to the next FFR meeting, where we would continue discussing the films. The meeting was at my place. I knew I should take advantage of the opportunity. I asked Tom, "Can you fix my DVD player?"

We stepped into the living room.

"Where are you from, Tom?" He didn't speak like a native Nova Scotian.

"Winnipeg."

"I'm from the Prairies, too."

"Really? Where?"

After a long explanation of my Ukrainian heritage, I said, "Do you want to help with the garage sale on Saturday? I'll buy you a coffee if you come in the morning."

"Sure."

"What do you take?"

"Cream."

Tom and I talked for four hours at the garage sale. It was worth the sunburn. The next week, we had our first official date.

A month later, Tom and I met with Sam at her office. When he saw me, he kissed me. Sam asked, "So are you a couple now?"

Tom replied, "I would like that."

I replied, "That's good for me."

HEAT INTOLERANCE

TOM WAS THE TECHNICAL coordinator for a not-for-profit, artist-run centre housed in the CBC radio building at the corner of Sackville and South Park, just off Halifax's main drag. While the weather was warm we met every Friday for lunch. My morning assistant, a six-foot-tall man from Nigeria named Chuby, would pack a lunch under my direction and then wheel me to the Public Gardens, across the street from Tom's office. Tom would meet us at noon. Chuby would take an hour for lunch, and Tom and I would have an hour to flirt.

Tom asked, "Where do you want to sit?"

I chose the shade near the geese. As the sun moved across the sky, the patch of shade receded and after forty-five minutes I was in the sun. As I became hotter, I grew more lethargic and spoke less. When I did speak, my speech was slurred. I was drooping like a flower with my chin to my chest. If someone held my head up, I could tell them I was fine and it was the heat that was getting to me. But Tom and I had only been dating for a brief time and he didn't know what to do.

Heat tolerance is characteristically absent in people with multiple sclerosis. I should probably just stay inside between ten in the morning and two in the afternoon, or wear a hat. But, when I think of wearing a hat, I immediately picture my grandmother's gardening hat or my mother's wide-brimmed straw hat. I'm still young. I don't want a hat like that.

Mother Barb Morris and Jen walking in Halifax Public Gardens, spring 2015.
(photo courtesy of Snickerdoodle Photography)

When Chuby came to take me home he found me slumped over in my chair with a worried Tom next to me. This heat intolerance was new to both of them. I knew the heat bothered me, and I should have moved into the shade. To make it home, we used one of my scarves to tie my head to the headrest of my chair.

A week later, my heat intolerance appeared again. A block and a half from home, I started to droop. Vidya was working that day. She didn't handle it as well as Chuby had.

"Jen, are you okay?"

Because my head hung forward, I couldn't answer her.

She clutched her hands. "Who can I call, Jen? Should we go to the hospital?"

She had stopped the chair in the full sun, so my condition only worsened as she freaked out.

"Should I go into one of these houses? Jen, answer me!"

I wanted to scream, "Hold my head up and I will answer you!" but I couldn't.

After a few minutes of fretting, she finally thought to hold my head up. I could feel the sweat trickling down my brow. I squeaked out, "Just take me home."

Once I was in the cool, dark condo, my abilities flooded back. I could talk like normal. I could hold my head up unassisted.

Vidya had only worked for me part-time for a few weeks. She couldn't have anticipated my reaction to the sun. I should have warned her what might happen. Soon after, Vidya asked me to give her a reference. I was happy to do so.

HOPE

On our first date, Tom and I had a conversation about disability. His eyesight wasn't great but he didn't wear glasses. He maintained he could see distance with the right eye and nearby with the left. The adjustment his eyes had to make through glasses annoyed him, so he chose not to wear them.

"Doesn't it bother you that you can't see far?" I asked.

"I see well enough," said Tom.

"But how do you ..." I remembered Tom didn't drive.

"My vision is good enough for what I need," he said. "If I start to get headaches, then I'll look at getting glasses."

With enough electronic medical equipment to put the Bionic Man to shame, I asked Tom how he felt about my dependence on technical aids.

"That's different," he said. "You need them to function like I need insulin to survive."

Tom has type-1 diabetes and takes insulin every time he eats. Tom hopes that one day there will be a cure for diabetes, but he knows it will not come in his lifetime. I feel the same way about multiple sclerosis. Many people with multiple sclerosis hope for a cure. I hope one day there is a cure, but I place more hope in treatments to alleviate pain and suffering. I only want hope if it's based in reality.

On November 2, 2010, I entered the provincial legislature

Tom Elliott and Jen at conductive education session, spring 2010.
(photo courtesy of Beth Lynch)

building through the back door, the only accessible entry. The province had proclaimed it March of Dimes Conductive Education Awareness Day. I was there to speak at a celebratory gathering. A sea of scooters and power wheelchairs filled the lobby. I had unwittingly joined a rally to prod Nova Scotia's elected officials to fund coverage for Italian doctor Paolo Zamboni's controversial vein-clearing treatment.

My father had offered to pay $70,000 for me to undergo Zamboni's treatment. I could travel to a clinic in New York, where they would perform angioplasty: inserting tubes in the veins in my neck to improve blood flow. Zamboni theorized that blockages in certain nervous-system-draining veins in the neck contributed to the development of multiple sclerosis. He dubbed the condition chronic cerebrospinal venous insufficiency (CCSVI). My doctors scoffed at the treatment, but hundreds of people with multiple sclerosis, including Zamboni's wife, swore it helped. The differences were often small and subjective, but some felt it improved their quality of life.

Dad felt we should be more aggressive in pursuing a cure. I

understood wanting to feel better but I feared disappointment. I could have joined the 3,000 Canadian multiple sclerosis patients who tried the Zamboni treatment, but the procedure was risky, expensive and unproven. One person in the United States had died, another had been paralyzed.

I declined my father's offer. Seeking solace in an unproven treatment is wishing things were different. They aren't different.

Back in the legislature, the scooter and wheelchair drivers, all with multiple sclerosis, were united by the hope that treatment would help them regain their abilities. Their faces, lit from above, were hard-edged. Many of them were angry that the disease had stripped away the characteristics they thought were fundamental to their identities.

I ducked into the legislature's tiny elevator.

Groups of people with multiple sclerosis unnerve me. I don't feel that sharing a diagnosis means we have anything else in common. I attended only two self-help meetings over the twenty years of my illness. Maybe not going to the groups is about not wanting to be identified as a woman with multiple sclerosis. Though I have it, why should it be my defining characteristic?

I travelled one floor up to the Red Chamber, where I met my conductive education instructor Beth, the one who had asked me to speak. CE helped me retain a positive attitude and reduced the pain in my hands and legs. It wasn't curative, but it allowed me to work with conscious effort to alleviate some of my symptoms. Increased awareness could have CE recognized by insurance companies, reducing costs to participants and their families.

I had presented in the Red Chamber when I worked as a disability advocate. The oak panelling and red carpeting were regal. I was more excited than nervous. This excitement helped improve the quality of my voice. The adrenaline allowed me to pronounce more clearly.

I addressed the dignitaries and shook their hands.

Despite the province's lip service, CE is still not recognized as a legitimate therapy.

VULNERABLE

DURING ONE OF MIKE's shifts as an assistant, I was emailing in search of someone to stay with me at night for the next week to replace my roommate who would be away on holiday. As a student, Mike needed extra money, so he volunteered. "I could do that."

At ten o'clock Tuesday night, I turned to Mike, "I'm about ready for bed."

We left the computer and went into my bedroom.

"Do you want to sleep in your bra? Won't that hurt? I know my girlfriend doesn't like to wear her bras overnight," said Mike. Sensing my discomfort, he assured me, "I won't look."

I agreed. I gave instructions on how to take off my shirt. Because my arms were tightly held to my sides you couldn't just lift my arms and pull my shirt over my head.

"First we take off the right sleeve, then over the head. Then the left sleeve. I'm sure you know what to do with a bra."

In the middle of the procedure, Mike had his head turned and his eyes firmly shut. But his hands were cupping my breasts.

"Mike? You're feeling me up."

"I know. But, I'm not looking."

"I think what you're doing is worse."

He dropped his hands, and turned his head to face me. "I know," he said sheepishly, "but I promised I wouldn't look."

I didn't feel violated by Mike's hands — his touch was functional, not sexual — but it made me think about how vulnerable I am to abuse or neglect. Research in 2014 found that sixty-eight percent of women with disabilities had experienced abuse in the preceding year. Thirty percent of these incidents were sexual abuse. Another study documented that twenty-eight percent of abuse cases of persons with disabilities are attributable to people responsible for their specialized care needs.

I am vulnerable to abuse — physically, sexually and financially — but because I can't do anything independently, what alternatives are there to trust? I can't answer the phone to buzz them in, so my assistants know the door code for my building. They know my banking PIN from when we buy groceries. I am lucky not to have been taken advantage of by the many people who have entered my life.

Sometimes I can't schedule my assistants to fill all twenty-four hours in the day, so I may be alone for half an hour or an hour. I think about what would happen if the fire alarm sounded while no one else was around. There is a sprinkler above the closet in my bedroom, but would the stream of water be forceful enough to reach me? Would I die of smoke inhalation? If fire fighters came to rescue me, it is doubtful my soft voice would reach their ears.

With the sound of an assistant opening the door after running an errand, the fear that has been growing since the moment the door closed with their departure evaporates. Someone is home. I am safe. Without another person present I am helpless.

My male assistant Jont and I went to Victoria's Secret to buy some bras. I had never purchased anything from there before, so I needed to try on each of the bras I picked out. I approached a "bra specialist," told her what I was looking for, and she brought me a selection. When I asked to try on the bras, she was exceedingly polite while telling me that my assistant could not accompany me into the fitting rooms.

"I'm sorry but males are only allowed when no-one else is using the fitting rooms. We can book a special appointment if you'd like to return later."

"What? But I'm here now and I can't try on a bra by myself?"

"Don't worry, we're happy to help."

"But, my assistant can operate my wheelchair."

"He can take you into the fitting room but then he'll have to leave."

This concession may have been prompted by the fact that minutes earlier, while operating my chair independently, I rammed into a large display of bras.

I looked at her helplessly.

She continued, "Policy is policy. We do it so that the other customers feel safe."

The policy didn't sound very accommodating. Aren't the change rooms individual stalls? I know my assistant is tall, but he wouldn't peep over the wall. He'd only be there because I need help.

I must have looked unhappy because the bra specialist reiterated her commitment to service, saying, "Don't worry, we're happy to help."

She enlisted the assistance of her manager, but they were unsure of how to remove my shirt. I tried to tell them, "You take off one elbow and the shirt goes over my head," but they seemed scared they would hurt me. Instead, they decided to measure me over my shirt and try the bras that way. I was skeptical of their plan but grudgingly agreed.

Gender divisions had caused problems for me before. Airports and malls now have family bathrooms where males, females and transgendered persons are permitted in any combination, but many older buildings aren't as accommodating. I've had more than a dozen male assistants, and whenever we have to use a public washroom, we're faced with a dilemma. The partitioning of female washrooms into stalls ensures that a male visitor wouldn't see anything, but women seem more self-conscious than men. I could imagine how my grandmother would react if she came out of her stall to be greeted by a six-foot-three man. My male assistants and I always opted for the men's room.

The plan to try the bras over my shirt didn't work as well as the staff at Victoria's Secret had hoped. We returned my oversized purchases two days later.

"I'm calling with Jen Powley. She is on speakerphone with me. She received a letter from you in the mail and wanted to ask you some questions about her disability savings plan."

"Sorry, we need to talk to her independently."

"I have all her information and she's sitting right here."

I took that as my cue.

"Hi. This is Jen. I give my assistant, Kira, authorization. My voice isn't strong enough for you to understand."

"Sorry, ma'am, I didn't catch what you said."

"Exactly," Kira said. "That's why she needs my assistance."

"We need to talk to only Miss Powley."

"I authorize Kira."

"Does she have power of attorney?"

I didn't want to give my assistants power of attorney. My assistants are employees who come and go, not family who I want to have the ability to change my will.

"No, but Jen is right here."

"I need her to talk to me."

"Here I am. Kira will leave the room."

Kira didn't leave my bedside but the people on the other end of the phone didn't need to know that.

"Okay. Do you have your bank card?"

"Certainly," I said, as Kira fished it out of my wallet.

"I need the last eleven digits."

The card was blue with gold writing on it. It was impossible for me to decipher the numbers with my low vision. Kira signalled — she had an idea. She wrote the numbers in dark blue ink on white paper — big enough for me to see. I read them off slowly to the telephone-banking representative.

"Zero, five ..."

"I'm sorry ma'am. That's not the right number."

Out of the corner of my eye I saw Kira fuming.

"Let me try again."

I knew I had read the number exactly as it appeared. The man on the other end needed to listen more carefully.

"Zero, five …"

"Ok ma'am. That's right. Now I need your security code."

"Security code? I set up the account six years ago. I don't remember what security code I gave."

I answered the security questions correctly and finished with my business. Both my shoulders and Kira's fell forward with relief as we hung up the phone.

I understood why the bank was looking out for me, but I had arrived at a point where I needed to take chances. I needed my assistants to write down my passwords. If I were only blind, I could type them myself. If it were only my hands that were impaired, I wouldn't need someone else to read the passwords aloud. I deal with both disabilities and more. I know what I do is risky but I don't have any other options. I am scared I will be taken advantage of, but I would rather live than be in constant fear.

MY ROOMMATE LEFT FOR her morning commute. Home care left after they finished dressing me. I sat in my wheelchair in the kitchen watching the clock on the stove.

7:59. Kira will be here.

8:02. Maybe she's running a few minutes late. She's usually here at eight.

8:04. I hope she's okay.

8:06. It is Monday, isn't it?

8:08. Fuck, where is she?

A week ago, I had ordered replacement parts for my hands-free cell phone, the wiring having corroded on the device I had. The parts hadn't arrived yet. Most hands-free units require you to press a button before you can talk. My phone operated totally on voice commands. It was expensive but worth it for peace of mind. Unfortunately, since it wasn't in working order, it was useless.

8:09. Fuck.

My roommate wouldn't be home until six. My building had new supers, so there was no chance of Paul finding me this time. I would spend the next ten hours alone with my thoughts. No food. No water. No readjustments. My butt would ache. The pressure would build. My leg bag would overflow.

8:10. The door opened.

"Sorry I'm late," Kira said. "My alarm clock broke last night."

I swallowed my frustration.

"That's okay," I said. "Are you okay?"

A LITTLE DRYWALL

ONE SUMMER DAY, AS I rolled out the back door of the EAC, an unexpected cold breeze hit my face and sent me into a spasm. My head was thrown back. Because the forward switch is at the back of the headrest, the motion was the same as putting my foot on the gas. I shot forward. Thankfully, my assistant Brittney was attentive and turned off my chair before I hit the bench at the end of the back deck.

Brittney warned, "You know what might happen if you hit that bench."

"Slivers in my shins?"

"If the nails holding the bench ripped out of the deck you would fall five feet into the garden. You would get hurt. Badly hurt. I would feel guilty. I could drive the chair, you know."

I knew. My chair has two settings — one where I drive with my head using the three buttons in my headrest, and one where someone else drives using the hand control. But I liked to be in charge, even if it was risky.

I declined her offer but questioned whether I was being reasonable. I took risks because it made me feel alive. Like a teenager making her first attempts at independence, I demanded the right to fail. But, if something happened my assistant would feel responsible.

In windy weather my wheelchair performs fine, but I don't.

Jen with sister Candice Laws, her husband Matt Laws, and Jen's partner Tom Elliott at the Anna Leonowens Gallery in Halifax, NS, spring 2015.
(photo courtesy of Snickerdoodle Photography)

The wind against my cheek pushes my head against the headrest. I don't have the strength to hold my head up.

"Should I drive, Jen? It's windy out," asked Sonya, my new assistant. We were in the parking lot of a Capital Health administrative building. I had a volunteer board meeting.

"Windy enough that I won't be in control?"

I worried about driving off the ramp. To enter or exit my wheelchair-accessible van, there is a ramp that folds up on the passenger side. Near the top there was a two-foot drop.

"I think it would be safer if I drive," replied Sonya.

I rationalized that at a health board meeting I should take the option that would leave me less vulnerable. I reluctantly agreed.

A week later I was lining up my chair with my condo door. If I left the condo at a bit of an angle, I would avoid hitting the other side of the hallway head on and punching a hole in the drywall,

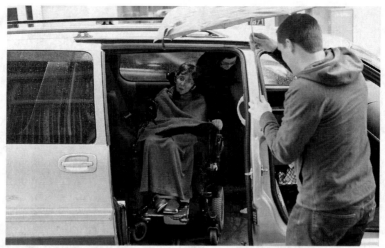

Assistant Liz MacBeth and brother-in-law Matt Laws directing Jen into her lowered floor van, spring 2015. (photo courtesy of Snickerdoodle Photography)

but I risked scratching the finish off the doorframe. The building manager had already spoken to me about that.

As I gave my chair a little power to get over the threshold, I had a spasm, the result of a temperature difference between my condo and the hallway.

"Turn me off!" I yelled to my assistant.

Flustered, Victoria fumbled for the on/off switch. My chair ceased moving forward, but my spinning tires told me it wasn't because she had found the switch. I knew that I couldn't be that close to the wall without the sharp footplate of my chair piercing the drywall.

"Too late," I told her. I asked her to see if I had made a hole in the drywall. I suspected I had but I hoped that I hadn't.

"There's definitely a hole," Victoria said. As she pulled me out, I noticed I was dropping little bits of drywall everywhere. I wrote a note and got Victoria to put it under the building super's door. The next day, a man was patching the wall outside the condo.

"I'm sorry," I said to the repairman.

"That's okay. It's good for business," he replied. "You've done this before, haven't you?"

Embarrassed at the reminder, I nodded. I had paid for new dry-wall and painting before. From then on I warned my assistants of what might happen as we left the condo and reviewed how to turn off the chair. I could get one of my assistants to drive, at the risk of having other people think less of me, but my pride was worth more than a little drywall.

I NEARLY DECAPITATED MYSELF during the holiday season. I was in Vegreville, parked at my mother's kitchen table. I moved my chair to look out the window. A spasm threw my head back, signalling to my chair that I wanted to move forward. My chair caught the edge of the table, pushing it up. The table hit my collarbone, then slipped up to my windpipe as the chair continued to advance. It was wedged between the wall and my throat.

With my weak voice I tried to yell to my mother, "Turn off the chair!"

If she couldn't, I would suffocate. Hearing the commotion, she raced in from the next room.

"I'm trying, I'm trying," she said, but the controls with the power switch had fallen to a place she could not reach. I wasn't ready to die. Thinking quickly, she pulled up one of the brakes at the back of my chair and I stopped. The table's advance on my throat ceased.

I burst into tears. She joined me.

HALIFAX WAS IN THE midst of March showers. One evening at half past six, when most people had already left work, Victoria and I were struggling to get to a presentation. I was scheduled to speak at an event in the Lord Nelson Hotel in half an hour. She and I found a parking meter a block away. I rolled down the ramp of my van and the front tires of my chair sank into the mud. Victoria wasn't strong enough to free 367 pounds of chair and a hundred pounds of me. I thought we could use the flaps from a box of pamphlets I had in the van to give us traction but they didn't give us enough purchase. There were people walking to their cars but no one seemed to notice our plight. Desperate for help, I searched my memory for someone we could call who would be close enough to rescue me. Finally, a well-dressed man in his fifties stopped and asked, "Can I offer you ladies a hand?"

We accepted.

"Why don't you grab the frame of my chair from the front," I said, "and try to lift it onto the sidewalk as Victoria pushes it forward?"

He pulled the chair almost effortlessly out of the mud. Once my chair reached the sidewalk the wheels gripped the surface and propelled me forward. We thanked our good Samaritan. Victoria threw my raincoat over me and we headed to the Lord Nelson.

KEEPING TOM

VERONICA OPENED THE FRIDGE door. "Where's the butter?"

"Just put salsa on it," I said.

Tucking an unruly ringlet behind her ear, Veronica said, "You know butter is the best."

"I don't really like the taste of it."

"How can you not like butter? You don't like cream either, do you?"

Veronica and I, employee and boss respectively, had the same secret. Both of us had dealt with eating disorders. Veronica appeared to be over hers. I still battled with issues of control.

In 2011, ten years after my four-month stint at the University of Alberta eating disorder clinic, my dietician told me I should put on at least ten pounds. I had slowly been losing weight. I didn't prioritize eating. If I was busy, I would miss a meal.

"It's for your own good. Think what would happen if you ever got sick," she warned.

My stomach was finally flat enough that it didn't bulge when I sat in my wheelchair. I could even tilt a little to change the pressure on my butt and my belly didn't look hideous.

Maintaining a younger-looking body was how I dealt with my fear of aging and being undesirable. My fight to maintain a healthy weight plagued me. I still counted calories. I didn't want to get older — not thirty-five, not forty. I desperately wanted to avoid the paunchy stomach that seems to come with middle age. By avoiding the look of middle age, I thought I could avoid becoming middle-aged. *Middle-aged* meant I should be an accomplished professional, financially self-sufficient.

These thoughts made me suspect that I wasn't fully over my eating disorder. My weight was less than eighty pounds. I could easily gain ten pounds and still be skinny. According to my dietician, then I would be healthier.

I knew I had a problem after a date night with Tom where I refused to brush the crust of a frozen pizza with olive oil. Eleven minutes after the pizza went in the oven, I asked Tom to check on it.

"The box says to cook it for thirteen," he protested.

"I know, but we should just check. There's no harm in checking."

Tom opened the oven and smoke rolled out.

"Shit," he said.

The smoke detector began to wail.

"Shit shit shit shit shit shit," he exclaimed, covering his ears. His perfect ears. Tom was a sound artist. He built sound tracks and soundscapes. He shut off the oven, grabbed a dishcloth and ran to the smoke detector. Standing beneath the screaming device, he flapped the dishcloth, trying to convince the alarm the building was not burning.

I was concerned the pizza was still cooking and envisioned the crust turning from black to charcoal.

"Tom, what about the pizza?"

Tom rushed back into the kitchen, reached into the oven and grabbed the pan with his bare hand. His perfect fingers. They were used to tapping out intricate rhythms.

"Daaamn," he shouted as he dropped the pan on top of the stove. He turned to the sink, ran the cold water and immersed his hand into the stream. He grimaced in pain but did not admonish me. He didn't have to. I silently blamed myself for wrecking his perfect fingers. I tried to convince myself that a little oil wouldn't have hurt me, but I didn't buy it.

While struggling with anorexia, I had avoided fats, be they olive oil, butter or something else. My insistence not to use oil meant that I wasn't fully recovered. But I wanted to be better. For three years after I returned from the eating disorder clinic, I was in group therapy. During that time, I saw my psychologist, Yvette, weekly. Seven years later, I scheduled a check-in with her. She listened in her usual accepting manner, then asked, "What is more important to you? The illusion of control you feel the eating disorder gives you or Tom?"

"Tom," I answered. I wanted to ask "Can't I have both?"

I'd managed to hold on to Tom for eight months even though I was still preoccupied with the amount of fat I consumed.

"I think you know what you need to do," she answered.

I knew what Yvette was implying. I had to choose between the eating disorder and a regular life. No one could do that for me. If I wanted a normal life, a life that wasn't consumed by counting calories, I had to forfeit the security of regulating what I ate.

ENGINEERING FAMILIES

HAVING HIRED TWENTY-SEVEN ASSISTANTS over eight years, I was accustomed to saying goodbye. Many of my assistants were students who didn't stay for more than the years they were in school. Others simply moved on. Working one-on-one with my assistants, I came to know them well, but they usually only knew each other through the emails they typed for me. Some of my assistants met at shift change, but if one worked on Fridays and another worked on Sundays, it was doubtful their paths would cross. Occasionally, I hosted barbeques for everyone who worked for me. Introducing themselves, they would say, "Oh you're blah-blah at gmail.com. I've read your emails." The barbeques were meetings of the Jen community. I would say "knees" — to signal that I needed to be repositioned — and four people would get up to adjust me.

I engineer families out of strangers, and in the time my assistants spend as part of my family, I hope they learn how strong someone who appears so fragile can be. I want them to go into the world as doctors, marine biologists, academics, librarians and artists who know that differently-abled does not mean dumb or ill-tempered. I want them to raise their children with compassion, and if their mother or brother ever needs assistance, I want them to know they are strong enough to step up and give it.

Scott worked for me part-time for a year and full-time for a summer. He was like a brother. I had a stepbrother whom I adored, but when I was growing up he lived with his mother and only visited his father, my stepdad, during school vacations.

Scott taught me about football, construction and accepting things as they came. Scott's parents adopted a baby girl when he was ten years old. His cousin had given birth to a daughter she didn't think she'd be able to look after, so his parents adopted the child. Scott went from being the baby to looking after a baby. Rather than shirking this new responsibility, Scott accepted it wholeheartedly. Just as Scott learned to be a big brother to his new sister, he learned to respond to my needs.

While working for me, Scott applied and was accepted to med school. When he came to say goodbye I was having a bath, which left my mother, who was visiting, to say goodbye on my behalf. "I hope you gave him a big hug," I said afterwards. Scott left me a card, which read:

Dear Jen,

Thank you for welcoming me into your home for the past year. It has been a life-shaping experience to work for you and I always looked forward to our days together. Your ability to put others first is inspirational. Your unwavering motivation to make your community a better place for everyone is an example everyone should strive for, but few can replicate. I hope you have continued success and happiness in your writing, art, work and anything else you attempt.

With Gratitude & Respect,

Scott

ANOTHER ASSISTANT, CHUBY, USED to lace his sneakers carefully. "That's the way my mom taught me," he explained. His mother had passed away from cancer two years earlier. He had come to Nova Scotia to complete a degree in petroleum engineering, a skill he thought would be useful in the oil fields of his native Nigeria. He tied his shoes deliberately, just like I imagined he lived his life.

Chuby and my assistant Henry nearly got into fisticuffs over the proper way to allocate oil revenues. Chuby thought that individuals had the right to the oil on their land. Henry, a Kenyan and son of a preacher, thought that oil revenues should stay with the state, where they could be used to benefit all citizens. The foyer of my apartment never seemed smaller than when their two egos filled the room .

"Too far," I said. My left temple was pressed against the head controller on my electric wheelchair. My assistant Sonya scooted to the other side of the chair. I sat on a hand towel. Pulling it one way or the other shifted the position of my hips. I requested just a little tug.

"How's that?" asked Sonya.

My temples were equally between the right and the left head buttons. If we had left my temple pressed up against the left side, I would circle endlessly when I tried to drive somewhere.

"Perfect," I said.

"How many times a day do you say that?"

"Say what?"

"Perfect."

"I want to make sure the people assisting me feel good about what they do. It's the difference between being part of the world and sitting around like a lump."

"I think we all know that you're grateful."

"But I want them to really know."

I'm consumed by the fear that if I'm not nice enough to my assistants they will abandon me, so I overcompensate. I've always had really high standards for myself. I think demanding other people conform to those standards makes me come off as a bitch. When someone is acting on my behalf, I have to adopt a different standard for them than I have for myself. My idea of "perfect" has decreased to "good enough."

MY VOICE

By the time I was seven, my forty-year-old Aunt Sylvia was in a nursing home. The doctors' vague diagnosis was of some kind of upper motor neuron disease. The strange smell of antiseptic and the expectation that I would behave well prompted me to avoid visiting Auntie Sylvia. But my reluctance ran deeper. The few times my father forced me to accompany him, I resented being there. The nursing home was so sad. There wasn't anything fun to do. There wasn't anything to do at all. I didn't understand what she did all day. There weren't any toys and her neighbours never wanted to play. When my aunt spoke to me, I didn't understand what she said. I felt sorry for her and I felt sorry for myself.

"What did she say?" asked Bob, an EAC committee member. I was giving an update at one of the monthly meetings for the Built Environment Committee at the Ecology Action Centre. I was humiliated, but I could appreciate Bob's problem. He had been in the military. The sound of exploding shells had damaged his hearing.

The head of the committee shook her head, admitting, "I didn't understand her either."

Now I was angry. What was her problem? She hadn't been in the military.

The issue with my voice wasn't only volume — it was also clarity. Communication skills were a requirement for the job I had.

When I was hired my voice was fine. Later, when I was forced to compete with the hum of lights and the whirr of a hectic office, I struggled. At least that's what I told myself. I was worthy of my job. I worked hard. But my contribution was limited by other people's ability to understand my speech. I'm lucky I didn't lose my job.

My rehab specialist referred me to a speech pathologist, who recognized my vocal projection limitations. I spoke softly as I lacked the lung strength to vibrate my vocal chords more forcefully. The speech pathologist ordered a personal microphone and speaker to boost the volume of my voice, but it made me self-conscious. I tried to tell myself it was like Madonna's microphone but I couldn't sing a note. I felt like a fraud.

The speech pathologist also referred me to a prosthodontist for a palatal lift. The muscles in my soft palate were failing. The prosthodontist fashioned a retainer with a scorpion tail that would do what my muscles could no longer do. After having the palatal lift fitted, I stepped out of the building and began reciting the alphabet to see if the lift helped. Things were going well until I got to K. I couldn't wrap my tongue around it. Q was also problematic. With time, I learned to pronounce them sufficiently. The best feature of the palatal lift was that no one knew it was there. Unless I tilted my head back, held my mouth open and pointed it out, it was inconspicuous.

First thing every morning my homecare workers put the palatal lift in my mouth so they could understand me. Routine pleasantries could easily be deciphered, but problems arose when I changed subjects. Assuming homecare workers wouldn't get my quirky comments, I stopped trying. I longed for my assistants, who started an hour later. They understood me.

I might ask home care for a *cream t-shirt*, but a worker might only pick up on *cr* and *shirt*, so I might get a long-sleeved crimson shirt. I don't argue with home care. I'd rather not embarrass myself by rehashing the conversation. I can deal with crimson.

My speech further deteriorated during the first three years of using the palatal lift. In 2010, Beth, my conductive educator, urged me to seek additional speech therapy.

The speech pathologist's office was overwhelmingly purple. The walls were purple, the folders were purple, the pens were purple, the chairs were purple. On the table in a purple box sat a stack of R words. When I was eight, I spent months in speech therapy because my R's sounded like W's. The first thing I told Dana, the young speech pathologist from Saskatchewan, was, "If I have to practise R's, like *roof* and *rooster*, I'm out of here."

"You won't need to do R's unless you want to," Dana said. "We could look at digital solutions to your voice problems."

I imagined staring at pictures of all my shoes, blinking twice to communicate which ones I wanted. I thought I was smarter than blinking to signify my desire instead of speaking. I thought people who rely on picture boards must not know their alphabet.

"I don't want to hear about it."

"There are many solutions that work with iPhones and tablets, but if you don't want to talk about it, just know that they exist if you ever do."

Dana recognized my limited breath support and suggested I break my sentences into chunks. I had been trying to speak my thoughts in a single breath. She suggested I share the address of the website for my project at work as: "www *breathe* dot ourhrmalliance *breathe* dot ca." Rather than drop sentence ends, she taught me to manage my breathing so my entire thought could be heard.

We worked on the letter H, produced by a strong exhalation. Dana told me Marilyn Monroe had been taught to speak breathlessly to combat her stutter. I was the opposite: I had to remember to inhale so I had strength enough to exhale. This was one of the tricks I could learn that would help me be understood.

Saturday was date night for Tom and me, and all week long I looked forward to our time together. For my birthday, he baked cookies stamped with the letter H in honour of my hard work, but they didn't improve my pronunciation. No matter how many I ate, I still couldn't exhale forcefully enough.

Five months later, none of the strategies Dana taught me were helping. Tom, who had perfect hearing, started to ask me to repeat myself. What if my lack of vocal prowess affected Tom's attraction to me?

I could think for myself, but I had difficulty letting the world know what my thoughts were. When I filled out my personal directive, my wishes for the course of treatment should my condition worsen, I noted that if I lost all ability to make my thoughts known — be it through speech, facial expression or blinking — I wanted to die.

I began to wonder how long I had before I wouldn't be able to communicate at all. I wasn't ready to die.

Familiarity was my salvation. People who knew me understood me. My voice was strong in the morning, crappy in the afternoon and returned around seven in the evening. For eight hours a day my multiple sclerosis won.

A year and a half later, I booked an appointment with Dana to look at the assistive devices. She invited a representative from Dynavox, an augmentative-communication-device maker. I knew I wouldn't want to hear what Dana and the representative had to say, so I invited Tom. His presence removed my edginess. In the meeting, the rep, Danielle, taught me how to trigger the computer by looking at different parts of the screen. I could make numbers and letters appear and the computer would say them aloud.

Controlling the Dynavox was thrilling. Triggering the Dynavox to speak for me wasn't the same as getting my voice back, but it was a voice. I started the paperwork to get financial assistance from the federal government so I could purchase the device.

The Dynavox we ordered finally arrived, and Tom set it up for me. The first challenge was that the screen needed to be at least eighteen inches from the end of my nose, and my eyesight is so weak that at that distance I had a hard time reading the menus. Tom started changing the font to a larger size, but the system seemed to demand that each page be changed separately. Although he spent hours fixing the font, there always seemed to be another page.

Tom set the screen to the calibration window. When I focused my eyes on a series of dots positioned across the screen, two cameras tracked my gaze. They should have been able to follow my eyes and know what I was staring at. I should have been able to stare at what I wanted to say, and the computer should have said it. It wasn't working. After trying unsuccessfully to get the speech-generating software to follow my directions, we decided to recalibrate.

"Maybe it's not seeing my eyes. Maybe we should try without my glasses," I suggested, knowing full well that without my glasses I had no hope of reading the screen.

Tom replied, "Okay love," as he removed my glasses.

I tried again, but even without my glasses, the cameras were having a hard time tracking my eyes.

"Tom, I don't understand what the problem is. It's eighteen inches from my nose. I'm right in front of it."

Tom said, "Can you keep your eyes open wider?"

I responded immediately, changing my expression to one of awe.

Tom said, "Look! The computer is seeing your eyes better." It worked, but I couldn't hold that expression for long.

"I don't get it. It worked so well with the sales woman."

I thought about it and realized that when I'd seen the company rep, it was first thing in the morning and I had slept through the night.

I emailed the rep about the problem and she responded promptly. "If your eyes aren't open wide enough the camera can't see your pupil because of your eyelid. But, if you want to try a different technology, there is a head mouse available. You attach a piece of reflective tape to your glasses and a camera can follow its movements."

I accepted her offer to send me a trial camera. It worked. It wasn't sexy, it wasn't perfect, but the camera could track my eyes. I could actually put a sentence together. It was like baby talk, but it worked.

I emailed her to ask how much it was. She replied, saying the camera cost about $700.

Not bad. I could ask for donations toward it as a Christmas present. In January, though, when I called to order it, the sales agent told me the final price would be $1700. I had a $12,000 machine that was useless without spending another two thousand to make it functional.

THE DIGNITY OF RISK

"Tom, can you put my head back on the pillow?"

My head had slipped off and I was finding it hard to breathe.

I expected his soft voice to answer, "Certainly." I expected his gentle hand to lift my head onto the memory foam pillow he had bought me for Christmas. I expected his usual concern and tenderness. Instead, he grunted. I knew his thumb was bothering him. It was infected and was a ghoulish purple-grey. I assumed he didn't want to hurt it further, even if his disabled girlfriend needed help.

I tried again, "Tom, I really need the pillow moved."

Another grunt. His perfect eyelashes didn't flutter with recognition. Now I was annoyed. Then it dawned on me: Tom's blood sugar must be low. Normal blood sugar is between four and six mmol/L. As a type-1 diabetic, Tom is totally dependant on insulin injections. At a four, Tom functions normally, but if his blood sugar drops below a four he reverts to the mentality of a six-year-old.

Fuck.

"Tom, your blood sugar is low. You need to have some juice."

Though we both appreciate the dignity of risk, I make sure there are two bottles of juice on the dresser every Saturday night when Tom and I have our weekly date. We operate with a chance of things not working out, but we don't take stupid chances. My doctor would advise me to have an able-bodied assistant at all

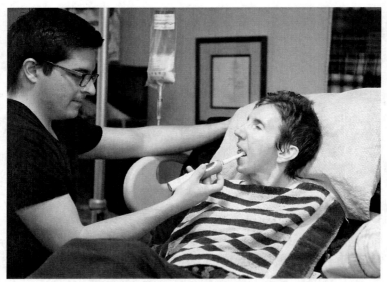

Roommate Ben DuPlessis brushing Jen's teeth with tube feed happening in background, spring 2015. (photo courtesy of Snickerdoodle Photography)

times. He might say I should be in a nursing home. I disagree. Tom disagrees.

I kept calling Tom.

"Tom! Tom!"

After about fifteen minutes of my desperate yelps, he turned his head slowly in my direction and opened his eyes.

He heard me!

Now I had to convince him to drink some juice.

Over half an hour, with lots of pleading, I convinced him to swing his legs over the edge of the bed, to stand, to grab a bottle of cranberry juice, to open the cap and to bring the bottle to his lips.

After Tom drank some juice and tested his sugar, he fell back asleep. The warm yellow light snaking out from the doorframe of my closet let me discern Tom's features — dark brown hair falling in ringlets over his expressive eyebrows. He looked peaceful. He was holding my hand and I felt his warm breath on my cheek. Given the inky blue of the sky outside my window, I estimated that it was 4 a.m. It wasn't close enough to morning for the birds to start chirping. Abie wasn't awake yet so there were no meows to remind us it was nearing her breakfast time.

I started to think about Tom's blood sugar and what would happen if he died in his sleep. I hoped I would pass away shortly after. Maybe my thoughts were less about Tom dying and more about me dying. Maybe then I would be comfortable going into "that good night," as Dylan Thomas labelled it.

I was tired of fighting. I was not in intense pain, but I was constantly aching and exhausted. When my conductive educator raised my arms to chest level at our weekly session, the spasms were so severe I cried out.

My decline was slow but steady. When I met Tom four years earlier, I had been able to touch my nose. Now I struggled even to scratch it, not with my hand, but by turning my head back and forth against a facecloth. I had to get Botox in my thumbs to stop them from digging into my palms. It's funny that a drug famed for making people beautiful is a treatment to keep hands from looking like ape claws.

I saw a documentary on Annette Funicello (one of the original Mouseketeers and a beach-movie star with Frankie Avalon). Like me, she had chronic progressive multiple sclerosis. Like me, her voice and motor function were affected. I didn't want to become what she was at the end of her seventy years.

Funicello seemed totally unresponsive. She was still loved by her second husband. As he talked about her, I could hear his admiration, "I talk to her and she understands me, she answers me, you know, in her own type of way." If that was true, maybe there was hope. Maybe Tom would be able to read me like Funicello's husband read her. But, I didn't want to live if I couldn't tell Tom I loved him.

I STOOD IN A black body suit and pink tights in first position at the barre, watching myself in the studio's mirrored wall. The piano music started. I extended my leg to the right, toe pointed, before I brought my heel to my ankle.

My internal metronome counted: and one, frappé.

I extended my leg again, striking the floor with the ball of my foot, inches before my leg was fully extended.

And two. I performed the movement again.

And three. Something was off. I was finding it hard to breathe. The movement wasn't strenuous. What was happening?

And four. I struggled to tighten my diaphragm to fill my lungs with air.

And five. I couldn't continue.

A movement from Tom woke me from my dancing dream.

CANADIAN DOCTOR MARK FREEDMAN has developed a treatment that shows some promise in halting the progression of multiple sclerosis using chemotherapy drugs to knock out a multiple sclerotic immune system. The theory is that when the immune system rebuilds itself it won't have multiple sclerosis. In trial cases this has worked, but the procedure is still being tested. I asked about the treatment at my yearly appointment with my neurologist, Dr. Virender Bhan. He explained that the chemotherapy can stop regression but it doesn't build anything you've lost. I have lost so much that there isn't much left to lose.

MY ASSISTANT BEN WEARS a Das Racist t-shirt depicting a headless Ali Baba on a magic carpet. It makes me think of Aladdin and what my three wishes would be if a genie were to appear. I might not wish to have never had multiple sclerosis, because it would mean losing all of the lessons I have learned. But I would ask for three specific things.

My first wish would be to play hopscotch on a warm sunny day with my nieces, Maddie and Ellie. I wouldn't be wearing shoes or socks, so I could feel the little pebbles on the concrete press into the soles of my feet. I would want to feel the sun's warmth radiating from the pavement — almost too warm to be comfortable. I would put my weight on one foot, then push off to land straddling squares two and three. I would hop to square four, feeling my leg muscles tighten and explode.

My second wish would be to walk along the edge of a warm lake. My feet sinking into the saturated sand, I would leave footprints but only for an instant. The movement of the warm lake water would nibble away at the indented earth. The sand under my feet would ooze into the groove where my toes meet the ball of my foot.

My third wish would be to wrap my legs tightly around Tom, then have existence come to an end with him in my arms.

My wishes granted, I couldn't go on knowing those experiences would again be out of my reach.

MOUTH DRAWING

I WAS ABOUT TO try drawing with my mouth for the first time.

"I'm scared, Tom."

He was sitting next to me at the dining room table. I used my mouth for kissing and eating but not for much else. I have long supported mouth and foot painters by buying their fundraising card packages, but I never thought I could be one of them. Tom and I had watched a YouTube video about mouth artists. We wanted to see how the painters held the brush. Holding a pencil in my mouth could work the same way. I just had one concern.

"What if I'm not any good at it?"

"Of course you won't be any good. You're drawing with your mouth."

He was right. Why did I have such high expectations? How would I be any good? It would be like picking up a trombone and thinking beautiful music would come out of it simply by pressing the mouthpiece to my lips. Tom's comment gave me the confidence to try.

Tom placed a pencil in my mouth. He held a coiled notebook firmly in front of himself.

Here goes nothing.

I didn't know what to do with the pencil. Should I hold it between my front teeth, or should I clasp my lips around it? I tried both. The pencil didn't even scratch the surface of the paper.

There wasn't enough force behind my head movements to mark the page.

I spat out the pencil. "Tom, I think I have to hold it in my back teeth. Otherwise I can't hold it firmly enough."

Tom held the pencil up so I could again take it into my mouth. I clasped it with my molars and then ... I made a line.

I made a line!

I tried again, crossing the first line. With practice, that could be an X. That could be a signature.

What if I could write a word? I started to print.

T — two lines. I can do this.

O — shit, a circle. Circles are hard.

Maybe I'd stick to T's.

I spat out the pencil. "Tom! Tom! Tom! Look!"

He grinned.

I could get good at this.

I began to worry about the enamel on my teeth. What if I wrapped the end of the pencil with tape? Masking tape tasted awful. Medical tape was better. What if I tried a different medium? A felt marker would mean I wouldn't need to press as hard. As soon as I clamped my back teeth onto it I could hear the plastic casing crack. With visions of blue ink staining my lips, I spat it out. Maybe I could try charcoal or watercolours or softer pencils.

I contacted an art instructor through Creative Spirit East, an art centre for people with disabilities. Andrea, my instructor, noticed that I could make very thin lines but thicker lines were a challenge. I spent a lot of time going over and over the same line to make it darker. She suggested powdered graphite. I hadn't even heard of that. If I dipped a Q-tip attached to a pencil in this stuff I could make more substantial lines. Later we switched to powdered charcoal for an even darker line.

Maybe it would never be good enough for an art card, but for friends and family it would be fine.

Using Tom as an easel couldn't last. I needed to be able to draw independently.

I called the Tetra Society of North America. Tetra, a non-profit organization, matches skilled volunteers, such as engineers, with people who need customized solutions to disability-related problems. They have an organizer in Halifax.

Two weeks later, an older man and his wife arrived at my condo. He had previously worked as a fish plant designer and operator. He looked at me and my chair and saw my limitations. Then his eyes widened. He took some measurements and promised to be back "lickety split."

A week later he was back with the easel he created.

He attached copper pipes to my wheelchair's armrests. The easel had two feet of smaller copper pipes that slid into them. The easel allowed me to draw with only minimal assistance. I needed someone to hand me the pencil — but I could create.

My assistant Jesse coordinated an art camp for seniors in a church that had donated the use of its hall. She held sessions every Monday morning and afternoon, modifying them according to the limitations of those who attended. In the morning, she had a group of active women who tried hula dancing standing up. In the afternoon, she had a mixed group who hula'd sitting down. She had asked Tom and me to attend as special guests to discuss how we made art.

Tom and I were given the floor as soon as we walked in. I thought a demonstration was the most effective way to show them the possibilities.

Tom set up my easel. "What should I draw?" I asked the group of sixteen participants.

"A flower," offered someone.

The members of the group nodded. I drew a quick flower. It wasn't intricate, but it was definitely a flower.

The next week Jesse told me how much my visit had meant to the class. Before, participants complained they were too old or too disabled to draw — they wouldn't be any good. After my visit these complaints stopped.

PRACTICAL

"How long has the power been out?" asked Tom.

"About half an hour. I waited to call to be sure it didn't come back on."

"Want me to come over?"

It was raining ice pellets. I felt guilty saying yes, but when there is a power outage the falling darkness unnerves me. Even Ajax pleaded with Zeus to let him die in the sunlight instead of the dark.

I hadn't been afraid of power outages as a child. Thunder and lightning terrified me but blackouts didn't faze me. I enjoyed the quiet. As my multiple sclerosis progressed, this changed. The hum of the refrigerator became an old friend.

I need power to pump air through the inflatable mattress I lie on at night to prevent pressure sores. I need power to recharge the batteries in my wheelchair. I need it to recharge my ceiling lift. I need it to open the front door. I need it to operate the phone. I need it for the baby monitor that connects my room to my roommate's. If the electricity isn't on, the systems I have in place to accommodate my disability fall apart.

"If you could come over, I would really appreciate that."

Charlotte was working as my assistant that evening, but she didn't provide the same sense of security as Tom. With Tom, I don't need to be strong. With Charlotte, I have to be the boss.

An assistant using the lift to put Jen in bed, spring 2015.
(photo courtesy of Snickerdoodle Photography)

When I am scared I can't step up to that role. Tom knows my fears and loves me in spite of them. Charlotte might think being scared of the dark made me weak.

THE CEILING LIFT, A motorized spindle running on a track along the ceiling of my bedroom, allows homecare workers to transfer me in and out of my wheelchair. A sling connected to the lift goes behind my back and under my thighs. With the press of a button I am raised into mid-air. I can then be positioned and lowered into place. I use it every morning. I feel the same way about it as I feel about my van. I appreciate when it works reliably, and it's stressful when the maintenance light goes on.

Mom refuses to use the ceiling lift to put me into bed. She compares the way I hang in the sling to a hunk of meat hanging in a butcher's shop. She prefers to cradle me in her arms, holding me close like when I was a child. From her point of view, carrying me into bed without the use of the lift is a demonstration of her affection.

I also prefer to be picked up and put into bed, but for utilitarian rather than sentimental reasons. Being lifted into bed is faster and easier — no sling, no straps, no pain in my arms when they are unsupported. When my mom or an assistant picks me up it is comfortable, but I don't think about it as being in someone's arms. It is only when Tom picks me up and we share a kiss and a hug that the transfer is anything more than practical.

Tom has few opportunities to put his arms around me. When I'm sitting in my wheelchair my back is against the custom-made, foam-filled backrest. When I'm in bed, I lie on my back or on my side and if he wants to hold me it means cutting off the circulation to one of his arms. But when we transfer into my wheelchair we sit on the side of my bed together. Tom holds me upright, and it is one of the few opportunities we have to really cuddle. A kiss is always part of the routine. He turns to me. I always ask for another kiss — which usually turns into two or three. His whiskers rub lightly on my cheek. His soft lips press on mine. I smell his musky scent as he pulls down the armrests and straightens my shirt.

WORKAHOLIC

"What would it look like if you were nicer to yourself?" asked Kira.

I was tired and I was in pain. I had sat all day and my right butt cheek throbbed. Kira thought I pushed myself too hard. My philosophy wasn't as accommodating. I placed too much pride in my work and community involvement.

Kira continued, "You work harder than a lot of able-bodied people."

She was not the first to point out how much I expected of myself.

One evening, my homecare worker Madonna was dressing me after a bath. We weren't putting on my pyjamas — we were putting on street clothes because I had a work meeting. Madonna noticed my arms weren't as flexible as usual. She knew that the tightness in my muscles, which held my legs and arms closer to my body, increased when I wasn't feeling well.

Madonna wasn't impressed.

"You're sick."

"It's just a cold. I'll get over it."

"Just look at you, Jen. You can barely hold your head up. You can't move your limbs. Of course you're sick. You shouldn't go anywhere tonight!"

I was afraid she was referring not to the cold but to my multiple sclerosis.

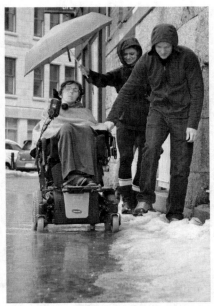

Jen progressing down Hollis Street, Halifax, NS en route to local gallery with sister Candice Laws and her husband Matt Laws, spring 2015. (photo courtesy of Snickerdoodle Photography)

"I'm not sick just because I have multiple sclerosis. I don't need to slow down."

Much of my stress is self-inflicted — a result of over-committing and feeling like I *should* do things whether or not I actually *want* to do them. When I make a commitment, I feel I owe it to other people to follow through. I'm afraid that if I stop doing what I do, I will start thinking about my pain and fatigue. My inertia will prevent me from starting again.

THE SYNTHESIZER

My assistant Brittney and I worked on the Seven Solutions brochure for the Our HRM Alliance. I started the initiative in hopes of changing Halifax Regional Municipality's master plan for development, to make it more environmentally friendly. I wanted stores you could walk to, better transit and more green space.

Brittney wanted to footnote the entire document like she had learned in university. While I acknowledged the value of citations, they looked clunky. I wanted the booklet to be slender and compact, with only essential information. We compromised. We included the references but no footnotes. The references were a huge hit, and I received more compliments on them than on the rest of the brochure. But, as I confided to Mom, I worried that the accomplishment wasn't mine alone.

"Mom, I don't deserve all the credit."

"What do you mean, dear?"

"Brittney deserves some credit. Instead I get it all and she isn't even recognized."

"How many assistants do you have working at a time?"

"I think up to eight. Six is average."

"You are the synthesizer. You bring the knowledge together with the skills. You are lucky to share a part of them but don't discount what you bring."

Mark Butler, the policy director at the EAC, had agreed to

co-coordinate the Our HRM project with me. The municipality's master plan was up for review, and I thought it needed massive changes. I thought if urban, suburban and rural groups worked together, municipal council couldn't ignore them. Our HRM Alliance was formed with me at the helm. Mark knew nothing about urban planning, but he knew how to run a campaign. He helped get funding for the project from Sage Environmental Program, Mountain Equipment Co-op and the Ivey Foundation. He used to admit at public presentations, "Jen is the brains behind this. I'm simply the voice." I was frustrated by my inability to lead a meeting. I tried to prep Mark as best I could, but it's hard to pack years of schooling and hours of research into a few brief sentences. I didn't know where to begin. The EAC was great about accommodating my special circumstances, but I felt guilty that I couldn't be a better project lead.

Part of the campaign involved informing municipal political candidates about our position on development. I met a candidate for council at a coffee shop downtown. The only available seats were high stools along the wall. This meant me and my wheelchair sat three feet below the candidate. My assistant had to repeat everything I said because there was no way he could hear my weak voice.

I gave a speech to alliance members at the provincial archives building. About halfway through my address, my voice gave out. Mark generously stepped in and tried to help me finish, but I was mortified. I couldn't do my job.

I looked into going back to school. I didn't need another master's, but at least I could pursue the degree at my own pace. At Dalhousie University graduate students are expected to work as teaching assistants, but I was sure I could work something out that wouldn't require me to embarrass myself every week.

I applied to a political science program at Dalhousie University and a creative non-fiction program at the University of King's College. I was accepted to both programs but chose creative writing because, although I didn't write a lot, I did have a degree in journalism and wrote for an online arts magazine, primarily for the free theatre tickets. I planned to write about the good, the bad and the ugly experiences I had with my assistants. Like the time I asked a new assistant if there was anything I could do to improve her job, and she replied, "It's not the worst job I ever had." She had spent the summer pulling entrails out of fish at a processing plant.

I would have to inform Mark and the rest of the EAC that I was going back to school. I wrote a resignation letter and emailed it to both the policy director and the internal director. Mark came into my office the next morning.

Without a *hello*, he said, "You can't."

"What?" I responded.

"You can't leave the project. It needs you. I need you."

"You'll find someone else who can do a better job than I can. I can't speak at meetings. That's incredibly frustrating."

"But I speak for you," said Mark. "Isn't that working?"

"It's working very well, but the project deserves more."

The Our HRM Alliance Steering Committee was celebrating with drinks and lunch at a downtown bar on a sunny day in August. Three years of meetings and strategizing were over. A new phase of meetings and strategizing was set to begin. I was proud that these business, health and environmental interest groups had been able to work together so seamlessly. I wouldn't be there for the next phase, but I had shepherded the alliance through the first one.

I watched as the director of the EAC hugged the head of the Downtown Halifax Business Commission. The lawyer, who worked in one of Halifax's prime downtown office buildings, shook the hand of a do-gooder from St. Margarets Bay and patted him on the back. While the camaraderie went on, I was sitting at a table with one board member and my assistant, feeling like I wasn't part of the party.

Maybe it was because I looked so fragile, couldn't reach out for a hug or joke with them because of my impaired speech. Maybe it was because I have so much electronic equipment around me when I'm in my power chair that no one can figure out the logistics of how to embrace me without being awkward or trespassing some boundary. I imagine friends and colleagues thinking: how do I hug around the chair? Where do I put my arms? Do I pull her forward? Will I hurt her?

I had been dubbed the "Godmother of the Alliance." Members of the Steering Committee kissed me on the head, ruffled my hair and went back to their conversations. They respected me, but I think they were afraid of disrupting some unspoken social contract.

I knew that Mark was comfortable with me when he sat down and rested his feet on the footplate of my wheelchair. It was the sort of comfort you find between old friends. The sort of comfort that took years to develop. Like someone resting their hand on your knee or touching your shoulder in conversation. It was not a comfort that many shared with me.

OF MY DECLINE

MOST PEOPLE DON'T GIVE swallowing a second thought. If I don't concentrate while eating, the results could be disastrous. My dietician had recommended a swallow test. She and a speech pathologist watched an X-ray monitor as barium-laced food lurched down my throat. The test confirmed what I had told the dietician: I had difficulty swallowing. She diagnosed me with dysphagia. My epiglottis wasn't moving fast enough to prevent me from choking on liquids. I couldn't swallow hard enough for crumbs to clear.

The dietician suggested I get a permanent gastric feeding tube (a G-tube). It wouldn't go up my nose (a very painful situation I'd just experienced when hospitalized for pneumonia), but directly into my stomach through a hole in my abdomen. I would still be able to eat normally but this way I could supplement my caloric intake without the risk of choking. My mother and Tom encouraged me to get the surgery, but I was dragging my feet. I found it hard to accept.

I wasn't sure how Tom would react — I still had the memory of Miles and his reaction to my catheter. There was my lingering eating disorder. A feeding tube would make it hard for me to deny intervention — I couldn't clamp my teeth shut and refuse to eat. Then there was the care of the tube itself and the implicit admission of my decline.

The main reason for my reticence was that I didn't want to give up cooking with Tom. It was a mainstay of our date nights.

Tom said, "What we do isn't important. It's that we're spending time together."

"But we always cook on Saturday nights," I whined.

"Things will change as they have to."

And they did.

Tom was feeding me lunch while we dined with one of my old assistants. As I drank cold tea, I inadvertently laughed.

I sputtered, liquid moving towards my lungs. Tom pulled my shoulders forward and thumped on my back, determined to prevent me from choking. I did not protest, knowing this calmed his nerves. He felt helpful. I didn't have the lung strength to cough so I tried to make a sound.

"Ahhh."

Tom had my tea ready to give me a sip.

"Are you okay?" he asked. "Do you need me to do anything?"

I told him I just needed some space. I would be fine.

That night I lay awake imagining:

"Hello, 911. My girlfriend is choking! She was eating and now she can't breathe!"

"Can she make any noise?"

"She can't breathe! Her lips are turning blue."

"What is your name, Sir?"

"She can't breathe! She can't breathe!"

"Sir, what is your name?"

"Tom, but ..."

"Tom, you have to remain calm. I'm sending an ambulance."

That image was enough to convince me. I chose to get the feeding tube on one condition: I wanted to maintain the option of not eating. Tom and my mother agreed to ask me monthly if I still wanted to live.

BREAKING THE ICE

WITH CHAIRS CIRCLING WHITE-CLOTHED tables, the room could have belonged to any conference. I parked in an open spot. I'm used to being the only power chair in a room, but here there was at least one power chair at each table. Their users were crippled: arms hyperextended by spasms, constantly moaning, heads thrown back.

It was the fourth bi-annual Breaking the Ice Conference in Toronto, for users of speech-generating devices — like Stephen Hawking.

The waiter seemed oblivious to the special nature of the diners. I wasn't.

I had to leave.

Tom and I ate at an Indian restaurant on Dundas Street, a block and a half away. Tom didn't ask any questions about my agitation.

That night I lay awake, troubled by my self-image. I remembered when my mother, sister, nieces and I ventured to Halifax's Discovery Centre. After Maddie and Ellie finished playing in the bubble room, our entourage headed to the wall of mirrors. Some mirrors made us fat, others skinny.

"Look at how much my ankles bow out in this mirror," I exclaimed. Mom stood beside me. She looked normal. The mirror wasn't curved. I asked Mom, "Can we make a strap to hold my legs straight?"

The pains I took to appear "normal" dominated my thoughts. I should have been sleeping, but instead I was reviewing how I made sure homecare workers always put my sweater over my seatbelt. I dressed in work attire every day, whether I was going to the office or not. I might not have the muscle coordination to actually walk but I didn't want to look like it was impossible. Maybe I was fooling myself. Maybe others saw me the way I saw the other power-chair users in the banquet room. I didn't want others to think of me like I used to think about Aunt Sylvia when I was six.

After seeing the others in that banquet room, I realized how futile my efforts had been. I could not hide the fact that I depended on a 367-pound power wheelchair. The general public would lump me in with other persons with severe disabilities. Even I had assumed that persons who were so disabled they didn't speak weren't smart enough to speak. And by now, I was having problems talking.

The next night, after a day of sessions and workshops, the organizers moved the tables aside to clear an area for a dramatic production. A group of volunteers dedicated to involving people with disabilities in theatre had written the first two scenes of a play entitled *The Journey at Sea*. Conference participants created the action in the third scene, set in a bar on an island closed off to foreign visitors. I imagined pirates.

Eight able-bodied actors and sixteen speech-generating-device users, including me, participated. Tom started alongside me, but fell back and took a seat in the audience. I was more comfortable with the assistants and professionals than with the other speech-generating-device users, but I wasn't horrified by them, as I had been twenty-four hours earlier.

ENVIOUS

THE CBC OVERNIGHT RADIO programming indicated it was four in the morning. I could put up with the pain in my arm for another hour, but I couldn't wait the three hours until home care arrived at seven.

My old roommate Liz had moved on. She wanted her own place. Kylie, a master's student who was friends with my conductive educator, needed a place to live. Since she was on a budget and I needed a new roommate, it worked perfectly.

Part of Kylie's job was to turn me at night if I woke in pain. I opened my mouth to call her but couldn't bring myself to say a word. I knew she was so stressed by papers and assignments that she needed her sleep. Maybe, rather than calling her, I could move my arm myself.

I tried using CE techniques to initiate movement with my left shoulder. I had been going to CE classes weekly for two years. I envisioned the movement and talked my body through the action. My left hand moved about a millimetre. It only provided temporary relief.

I would have to call Kylie. I gave her a room and a supplement from the Department of Health to compensate her. I shouldn't worry about bothering her. It was her job to look after me overnight. But I felt guilty all the same.

She had a look of "I told you so" when she walked into my

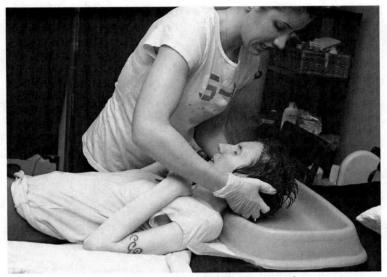

Homecare worker Jillian washing Jen's hair in a tray. This type of tray is affectionately referred to as a banjo because of its distinct shape, spring 2015. (photo courtesy of Snickerdoodle Photography)

bedroom. Before I went to sleep, she had said the placement of my arm looked odd and I probably wouldn't last the whole night in that position, but my arm had felt fine. I suspected she was right, but I didn't know what else to do. I had to come up with my own solutions for my problems. I worked by trial and error. Sometimes my solutions worked and sometimes they didn't.

With multiple sclerosis, each day is different: what has worked in the past doesn't necessarily work in the present. I can't explain why I can squeeze Tom's fingers today but couldn't yesterday. I don't know why some nights I sleep all night in one position, and other nights I need to call my roommate two or three times.

Kylie walked out the door with a single backpack. "Have a great weekend," she yelled.

One little bag.

One little bag to hold everything she needed for a weekend. I need a suitcase for an overnight stay. I can get away with a medium-size one but if I really want to be prepared I should use large.

I need an inflatable mattress and a motorized air pump to continually circulate the air in my mattress. The last time I went without it, I had to wake my roommate every half hour to reposition me.

I need a wedge to keep my upper body elevated to prevent choking as I do a tube feed. A gravity-dependent bag, a connector tube and a syringe to use for feeding. Q-tips and Polysporin to use for cleaning around the G-tube site.

I need two sets of pyjamas and weekend apparel in case I pee myself.

I need a container to drain the urine from my leg bag, an irrigation tray to remove any blockages, another catheter to replace the original in case of hopeless blockages and diapers as a last resort.

I need incontinence pads: cloth on one side, vinyl-treated on the other. They lie on top of the regular sheet to help turn me and to stop urine from soaking into the bedding and mattress.

If my trip is to last longer than three days or if we'll be walking more than a few blocks, I need to pack my five-pound chair-battery charger.

I need an air pump to add or remove air pressure from my seat cushion.

I need to travel with someone who is both strong enough to transfer me in and out of my chair without the aid of a ceiling lift and accustomed to undressing me.

If I pack my own supplies, I may be able to avoid a night in the emergency room.

After hearing that Kylie had left on vacation, my Jen-sitter Dianne asked, "If you won two tickets for round-trip airfare anywhere in the world, where would you go?"

"Alberta," I replied.

"But you've been there."

"I have, but all the equipment I need is there."

ROUND AND ROUND

"How do they stimulate your rectum?" the nurse asked. "Do they use a sweeping motion, or more of a round-and-round?"

I didn't know. I tried not to think about what the nurse was doing when he or she had their hand up my butt. Didn't they learn this in nursing school?

"Pardon? If you're not comfortable doing this I can wait for another nurse," I snapped. He was a registered nurse. Shouldn't he have known? When I called VON, I explicitly stated what I needed done.

"I was a military nurse for twenty years. We didn't get a lot of quads. I'm worried I'm going to hurt you."

Maybe the nurse wasn't inept. Maybe it had just been two decades since he had assisted a quadriplegic in performing a bowel movement — if he ever had.

I was lying on my side with my skirt around my waist, butt revealed. I had taken an oral laxative the night before to bring my stool into the lower rectum. Now, it needed to come out. I needed the nurse to perform a manual bowel movement to scoop the poo away using a finger up my anus. I had lost the ability to push my own stool because of my impaired nerve function. A butt full of shit is uncomfortable. To cut the tension, I joked with the grey-haired military nurse, "Better out than in."

I'd had big male nursing fingers up my ass before. With

lubricant, it didn't much matter. There were five nurses who regularly came to see me, but anyone trained in the procedure could show up.

After he emptied my rectum, I asked "How much return did you get?"

I needed to know how my body was functioning, and that included the amount of shit the nurse scooped out of me.

During another bowel-care session, I asked a different nurse about a liquid diet. I thought that maybe if I eliminated everything solid from my diet, I wouldn't need to shit.

"Even without eating any solids you would produce crap," she said.

I had no choice: bowel care had to be part of my routine.

My ability to remain in my home, rather than be forced into institutional care, is in part due to the VON. These visits allow for minor but necessary medical procedures to be carried out between my other productive tasks. I can have physiotherapy in the morning, have VON perform bowel care in the afternoon, then work on my university assignments. All this before evening home care washes my hair and changes me for bed.

Once a month, someone from VON changes my supra-pubic catheter, unless it clogs before the four weeks are over. When I had the initial insertion procedure, I asked the surgeon not to sew my urethra shut. I knew of a woman whose urethra had been sewn shut. She later had a blockage in her tube. Her bladder had no way to empty. It eventually ruptured and she died of septic shock. I imagined that the bladder rupture was terribly painful. If my bladder becomes too full because the catheter isn't draining the urine, my sphincter will release and I will wet myself. It's not ideal but it's better than dying. At least, that's what I think most of the time. Other times, I think the woman who died knew what she was doing.

PUT A RING ON IT

CLICK.

"Tom? Are you there, Tom? Tom?" A dial tone was the only response. I lay in bed, the room an inky black. Only my nightlight glowed.

"Can we call him back?" I asked Kylie, who had entered the room when she heard the phone beeping through the baby monitor.

"Hello?" Tom answered in his husky voice.

I started to speak. He hung up again.

I thanked Kylie for her help and pondered the thing I had said to offend him.

I said I had fallen in love with another guy. He must have missed that the guy was a character in a novel.

Since I was a little girl, I had wanted to be married. I grew up thinking that if you loved someone you married them. I wanted the security of knowing someone was behind me if I fell. When my parents divorced, I assumed my father had fallen out of love with my mother, my sister and me. I resented my half-sister because my father chose her over my family.

Tom and I had talked about marriage in the past, and I had said I didn't want to get married. A strong, independent woman didn't need marriage. It was a passé idea connected with religion, and I wasn't attached to any church. Logically, I should be beyond wanting marriage, but I wasn't. I wanted to know Tom would always be there to catch me. I decided I wanted to get married and I was disappointed when Tom didn't give me an engagement ring for Christmas or Valentine's Day. But since I had told Tom I didn't want to get married, how could he have known otherwise? I decided to propose to him.

I put the ring under a book a former assistant had given me. It sat on my desk, near my bed, where I lay recovering from a pressure sore.

It wasn't the first ring I had purchased for Tom. I bought him a ring eight months earlier when I had gone into the hospital with pneumonia. I told him to wear it on any finger but his left ring finger. I could remember his hand running gently down my side, pausing at the indent of my waist. I was sure I was going to die, and he deserved something to remember me by.

Now I was ready for a commitment.

"Tom, can we read from the book on the desk?"

He picked up the book without even glancing at the desk.

"Tom, can you look at the desk?"

He looked.

"The box."

He found the box with the ring and opened it.

"Tom, will you quote unquote …"

"Yes," Tom interrupted.

I continued, "… marry me?"

He committed to being with me, but in Tom's eyes, signing a marriage document made us part of a bureaucratic nightmare. Before we signed any papers, he wanted to ensure that we did not take a step that would affect the support I received from the provincial government. Home support is income tested, and if our combined income was more than $39,000, the province wouldn't cover it.

I knew our marriage wouldn't look typical: our finances would remain separate, our schedules would be different, and we wouldn't occupy the same living quarters. I had asked Tom to move in with me more than once. I asked every time I needed a new roommate. Each time I asked, he refused. He said he needed his space.

I still wanted the commitment. When I proposed to Tom, I announced, "I love you more than I imagined loving anyone."

At one of Tom's work events, I told a woman I used to work with about the engagement.

"You asked *him*?"

I nodded.

She said, "I should have predicted that."

I never dreamt of a wedding with a white gown and three identically adorned bridesmaids. Many marriages seemed to be more about the party than the commitment. I didn't want a party — I wanted the vows.

SUICIDE

THE SUICIDE RATE AMONG people with multiple sclerosis is seven and a half times that of the general population. Fifteen percent of multiple sclerosis patient deaths can be attributed to suicide. If I were to commit suicide, I would be reduced to a statistic.

In the town where I grew up there was a man without a nose — the result of a failed suicide attempt. I was afraid of screwing up if I tried to kill myself

I knew of a man who committed suicide. He was described as "too profound for the life he had been given." I want my epitaph to be weighty too. I fear if I do commit suicide I will be written off as a woman unable to cope with her multiple sclerosis. I don't want my disease to define me.

But I still think about suicide.

I figure driving my chair off a curb into the path of an oncoming transit bus would be the best option. It would be quick and painless. But I wouldn't want to cause a bus driver to unwittingly commit manslaughter. There is also the problem of what my chair would do if I drove it off a curb. I've never attempted a six-inch drop. Would my chair fall forward? That's the only way the bus plan would work. If the chair fell to the side or got stuck with the front wheels down and the back wheels on the curb, a collision likely wouldn't kill me.

Plan B is to drive down a staircase at full speed. It could be written off as a spasm that threw my head back against the gas pedal in my headrest. Investigators wouldn't know if the fall was intentional or an accident.

A PICTURE FOR TOM

I PARKED SO THE windows were at my back. The morning light was good for drawing. My drawing lessons were always first thing in the morning, when I had enough energy to sit up straight.

"The eye looks great," said Andrea. "The black pastel really makes it stand out. Why don't you add more?"

Not long after I started mouth-drawing with Tom, I enlisted Andrea to work with me. Andrea had never taught mouth-drawing before, but her patience and willingness to find alternate ways to draw suited me well. She had guided me through my two other drawings: a platypus for my sister in Australia and a pair of clasped hands for my mother. Now she was guiding me through a picture of a giraffe for Tom — a tribute to a plastic giraffe he had bought for me.

Andrea continued, "What if we darkened the spots and the mane and the shadow on the ..."

"You want me to use more pastel?" I interrupted.

"It has an amazing effect."

It was amazing, but it was also only a matter of time until I screwed up. I knew I would shake my head and make an errant mark. When I attempted pastels on the giraffe before, I covered the drawing with scrap paper leaving only the eye visible. With charcoal, my usual medium, you could erase. Pastel you could lighten but not remove. It was like life — screw-ups left their mark. That was why I didn't create with watercolours: there were only so many

The picture for Tom. It was inspired by a plastic figurine that Tom once got for Jen. Jen's niece, Maddie, aptly named it Ginger Spotty Longneck.

birds I could add to a skyline where I accidentally made a mark. I couldn't put a bird behind the giraffe.

I had worked so hard on this picture. If I made a huge dark line across the paper, there wasn't time to start again. I was having surgery in fifteen days, and I needed to finish the picture before then. Tom would love whatever I gave him, but I wanted it to be perfect. Tom deserved the best. It was best if I swallowed my fear and made those dreaded pastel lines.

My MUSCLE TONE HAD increased to the point that it was painful to attempt to pry my knees apart. My homecare workers had a hard time putting shoes on me because my big toes stood straight up. In my specialist's opinion, the solution was to insert a Baclofen pump under the skin of my abdomen. It was a hockey-puck-size reservoir for anti-spasm medication, which would be released into my spine through a plastic tube. The plan was to insert the pump while I was under general anaesthesia. Convinced the stress from the anaesthesia on my weak lungs would kill me, I verified that my living will was on file at the hospital. I made it clear I did not want to be resuscitated should my heart fail.

My mother arrived in Halifax the morning of my surgery. She met me at my condo. I asked for a hug as soon as she walked through the door.

"How was the flight?" I asked, adding, "Thank you for coming."

"I wouldn't miss it."

"I appreciate how you raised me."

She looked at me with confusion.

"I think I'm going to die, so I wanted you to know."

"You're not going to die. They wouldn't do the surgery if you weren't strong enough for it."

"The drawing I made for Tom is in the tray on the square table in the living room."

She retrieved it and exclaimed, "It's beautiful. He'll love it."

"Will you frame it and give it to him if I die?"

"You're not going to die."

"But will you?"

"Of course. But, you're not going to die."

After check-in at the pre-op desk, Tom, my mom and I made up stories to entertain ourselves.

"Tom," I said. "Make up a story using wallpaper, rubber boots, a canary and the action of painting. You can use two characters: yourself and an eight-year-old boy."

Tom asked, "Can I write that down?"

Mom dug in her purse for paper and a pen.

When I was called to pre-op, my tension level increased. I wasn't ready to die. I still had to finish writing my book. In the many years of living here, I still hadn't seen the sun rise over the Atlantic. I wanted more nights with Tom.

We tried to alleviate some of my dread by talking about other things. The nurse made me lie on a gurney, stripping me of my power wheelchair, taking away my ability to move independently.

"Tom, do you think you could lie next to me? I'm pretty small and the bed is pushed against the wall, so I won't fall out."

Embarrassed that I would suggest such a thing with my mother present, he replied, "I don't think that would work."

"I think we could make it work."

"Jen, I don't think it would be safe."

"But I want to feel your arms around me one last time."

"There will be other times. You'll be fine. They wouldn't do the surgery if they didn't think you were strong enough to handle it."

In spite of my fear that I would die on the table, I had referred to the procedure as "minor" in the weeks leading up to it. During the consultation that morning, the surgeon explained they would push the tube delivering the medication into the spinal column, under the vertebra and under the dura and pia mater. I had thought the tube would end near my spine, not actually in it. Hacking into the spinal column is not minor. In my head I reclassified the procedure.

Six hours after the consultation with the surgeon, I met with the anaesthesiologist, a German man who had read my file diligently.

"I don't think your lungs are strong enough to deal with general anaesthesia," he said. "I would be more comfortable using a sedative and a series of local anaesthetics."

My heart swelled. Finally, someone shared my concern. Now all I had to worry about was the procedure itself.

A few minutes later, the nurse informed us they were ready to operate. I turned to Mom and Tom thinking it might be the last time I saw them. Mom gave me a big hug. Tom kissed me and I felt the warmth of his lips.

"I love you, Tom. Thank you for our time together."

"There'll be more times," he said.

I was wheeled into the neurological operating room and surrounded by an army of nurses gearing up for the operation. The first thing they did was turn me on my left side and tape me in place so that I wouldn't move. I felt like the contents of a box looking up to see the lid being taped down. The surgical staff, all in blue gowns, passed the roll of tape from hand to hand. The last thing I remember was seeing them put up a blue sheet between my head and my body so I couldn't watch even if I were awake.

I woke up to a nurse checking my vitals in a small recovery room. The only light was from the hallway.

I made it.

I was so certain I would die I hadn't given any thought to the possibility that I might survive. I was confused about whether I should be happy that I made it or disappointed that my struggle wasn't over. If I had died on the operating table, I wouldn't have any more time with Tom, but I also wouldn't have to deal with any more doctors telling me I would continue to get worse.

Before the surgery my knees were always bent at ninety degrees. When I lay down, my knees stayed bent like I was sitting in my wheelchair. Now, my legs were almost straight, but unless I put a pillow under my calves to support them, my knees ached.

Before the surgery, my elbows were bent as well. An occupational therapist asked me why I didn't use the armrests on my chair. She thought having my arms farther away from my sides would force me to push out my chest, allowing me to take bigger breaths, increasing the volume of my voice. What she failed to understand was that my arms were held too tightly to my sides by my tone for my elbows to reach the armrests. After the surgery, my arms could reach the armrests, but I wasn't used to that position and it left me feeling exposed. I prefer my hands sitting in my lap, my arms forming a shield.

Before the surgery, my body may have been contorted but it was mine. I could feel Tom grab me around the waist. It may have been tricky to pry my legs apart but with proper instruction and patience, it could be done. I didn't realize the medication released by the Baclofen pump would change all that.

I used to turn over by having someone pull one of my knees.

The rest of my body would follow in a single motion. Now all the effort did was move my knees apart.

Sarah, one of my homecare workers, asked, "How does it feel? It must be so nice."

I wanted to scream, "If you could take this goddamn pump back and leave me with my normal body, I would happily switch!" Instead, I mumbled something about how different it was. The physical therapist told me I would like my new body. I just had to give it time. I did like that my fingers didn't cut into my palms, but I didn't like that I was no longer able to sit up all day.

Before the surgery my muscles were so contracted that it took very little energy to sit. Now I had to work to hold myself up, and it was exhausting. Before, I could sit up from eight in the morning to ten at night. Now, I was lucky if I could do eight to noon. I knew that eventually I would think of this new body as my own but the transition was exasperating.

Two days after I got home from the hospital, I took a laxative in preparation for VON's bowel-care visit the following day. It worked faster than expected. I asked my mother to clean me up. It didn't go well. At the end of it, my mother said, "It would have been better if you hadn't had a bowel movement until tomorrow."

My eyes welled with tears. Saying "it would be better if" floored me. So many situations "would be better if." It would be better if I didn't have multiple sclerosis. It would be better if I could go to the washroom myself. I looked at her and said, "I can't live by 'it would be better if.' I have to deal with what is."

REACTIONS

To be true Nova Scotians, I thought Tom and I ought to see the vibrant yellows and rich reds of fall in Cape Breton. I had travelled the Cabot Trail once before, but that was in August when everything was still a summer green. Ben and Liz, my current and my former roommates, completed our travel team. I arranged for us to travel to Sydney and then to Keltic Lodge near Ingonish. We ate Thanksgiving supper in the dining room at the Lodge.

The server was talking to Liz. I couldn't hear what she was saying. My attention was trained on Tom. I noticed something was off.

"Tom?"

No response.

"Tom? Can you hear me?"

No response.

I thought from his silence that his blood sugar was low. He had told me a month before that he always wanted to check it before he drank something sugary to raise the levels in his system. I thought it was beyond testing.

I interrupted the server, "Could we get some orange juice, please?"

She scooted off to fulfil my request.

I was concerned about Tom. Liz knew better than to interrupt my fretting no matter what her news was.

The orange juice arrived in a glass mug.

Reading in a children's room of the Central Library, Halifax, NS. From left to right: Danny Dodds, brother-in-law, Ellie Dodds, niece, Barb Morris, mother, and Jen, April 2015. (photo courtesy of Snickerdoodle Photography)

"Tom, drink."

"Tom, please drink the juice."

He trusted me and gulped it down.

Within a few minutes he returned to normal. Once I was satisfied the crisis was averted, I turned my attention to Liz.

"What was the server talking to you about?"

"Oh," she exclaimed, leaning in so all of us could hear, "she said another customer wants to pay for our supper!"

"Who?" I asked.

"Well, she wouldn't say. She wouldn't tell me if the guest was still here or even if they were male or female. I guess the donor wants to remain anonymous."

"Wh-what?" I stammered.

"She just said a donor would like to pay a hundred dollars of our bill."

"Really?"

I was surprised. A well of emotions bubbled up. I wanted to feel grateful but I didn't like being an object of charity. I wondered what inspired our donor to act. What motivated them? Are people with disabilities so uncommon in the outside world that they should be rewarded for leaving their homes? Was this someone's way of thanking the world that their own children were healthy? Did they have a relative they wished they could help more? (I could see my sister acting in the same way.) Were they amazed by my friends, who were obviously taking such good care of me? I felt guilty that the gesture raised questions rather than thanks. If only my guilt would subside, I could appreciate the gift, but without knowing the donor or their motivation, I was afraid it was born of pity.

Tom and I were going to our respective family homes for Christmas. He was flying with me to Edmonton. The muscle over my butt bone was damaged from repeated pressure sores and would never be as strong as before. To be comfortable, I had to sit at an angle, shifting the weight from the front to the back of my pelvis. Usually I achieved this by tilting my wheelchair but on the plane, the seat was stuck at near ninety degrees. I felt like someone was punching my right butt cheek. Hard. Continually. I started hoping the plane would crash to put me out of my agony. To take the pressure off my ass, I lay on my side across Tom's lap.

Looking across his knees to the space under the seat where lighter personal items were stowed, I saw only darkness, then a single iridescent drop of saliva. I was drooling. I don't normally drool but in this position I couldn't close my mouth to stop the saliva from leaking out. It landed on the carpet. I hoped they disinfected between flights.

"Tom, unhhh, unhhh, unhh."

He took my mewling to mean I wanted to sit up. I did not. The pain that had subsided for an instant now returned. I tried again.

"Tom, unhhh, unhhh, unhh."

"Sorry, dear, I can't understand. Can we try again?"

"Tom, unhhh, unhhh, unhh."

Tom shook his head in frustration.

"I'm trying to understand but I can't hear you over the roar of the engine. I have an idea," he said.

Tom suggested writing out the alphabet on an air sickness bag in five letter chunks. A B C D E was the first set, F G H I J, was the second, etc. Tom would read the letters in a row and I would shake my head yes or no to signal if the correct letter was in that row. He would then go letter by letter. He apologized for the crudeness of his system and how tedious it was. I was happy to be able to communicate at all. In a few minutes I was once again lying across his lap. Drooling was better than the agony of sitting.

Five long hours later, the pilot announced that we were approaching Edmonton airport. I was the last to deplane as they had to retrieve my wheelchair from the luggage compartment. I was transferred to a Washington chair to wheel me off the plane. It was harder on my behind than the plane seat, but at least I knew relief would come as soon as I could sit in my own chair. Forty-five minutes after the flight landed we emerged from the back hallways, the circuitous route wheelchairs take, to find my mother near the baggage carousel. A big hug and I was home.

It would be convenient if our desire to do things waned with our physical ability to do them. Accepting how things are rather than wanting them to be different has been my challenge. I have learned to operate from the part of my heart that is not full of the impossible.

When I was in Alberta, Dad visited me at my mother's almost every day for coffee. It was common for Mom's new partner, Joe, to join us. On the first day I asked my dad how he was doing.

"I'm still walking," he said. "Not in a wheelchair yet."

He didn't realise how comments like this made me feel ashamed, as if I had simply given up and liked to use a wheelchair.

After Dad left, I remained at the kitchen table with Joe.

"I couldn't live like your father does," said Joe. "I have to get outside, skiing down mountains and working. Your father goes the six steps from his house to the car parked in the heated garage, then drives to work, then takes another six steps from his car to the office. I couldn't live like that."

Joe's profession, a boilermaker, was physically intense. Joe couldn't imagine adjusting his life the way Dad had. I'm sure my father couldn't have imagined it either twenty years ago.

As his condition progressed, Dad had to sell his beloved farm and focus on his work as an accountant. My sister and I came from Australia and Halifax respectively for the farm equipment auction. Dad's balance was becoming increasingly precarious. He found he couldn't trust his body near the spinning blades of the swather and combine. He was lucky he still had all four limbs.

Neither Dad nor I made changes willingly. Our multiple sclerosis forced us to.

REFLECTION

THE QUESTION AT THE top of the handout was impossible for me to read. Even though it was bigger than standard font, my assistant Liz had to read it aloud to me. Though I should be used to it by now, I am embarrassed when someone needs to read to me. I want to yell out that I know how to read. My mastery of the English language is better than average. The letters are just too small for me to decipher. I want the world to know I am smart enough to know my alphabet. My broken body doesn't reveal the status of my mind.

That writing at the top of the page said, "What groups do you feel you belong to?" I was at a trans-ally workshop, but I wasn't used to thinking of myself as a sexual being, which is how I thought they wanted me to think of myself. The answer to the category question was obvious to me. I was disabled. People with disabilities in Western society are asexualized.

I didn't think of myself outside of being disabled. I "know" I am more than my disability, but it is only through interactions with others that I recognize that I can be more than disabled. When I wake up in the morning and have to wait for home care to dress me and put me in my chair, I am wholly disabled. When I have an assistant drive my wheelchair because my neck muscles are tired, it is disability that defines me. As I get my hair cut, I look in the mirror to see my stylist Michael holding up my head with his right hand while cutting with the left. I feel disabled. When I want to have a cough drop and no one understands the words coming from my lips, I comprehend why. The language is unfamiliar, not the words themselves but me saying those words. It's not anticipated. When I say "knees" or "nose" or "water" my assistants know what to do but with other people I am unintelligible. This highlights how disabled I feel.

But when I go to a meeting of Rainbow Refugees, a group that sponsors LGBTQ individuals from overseas, the people there know me as the president, not as someone who is disabled. The people I used to work with at the Ecology Action Centre know me as Kapow-ley, working hard to make Nova Scotia's largest city more sustainable, not as a person with a disability. When I go to a health board meeting, I am seen as a seasoned board member, not as a disability.

It is only with my partner Tom that I can see myself as sexual. There is no distinction between abled and disabled. We are only people, warm bodies in each others' arms.

I need to remind myself that I am not defined by my gross motor ability. Twice a year, my mother ventures to Halifax to spend a couple weeks of "quality time" with me. I use it as an opportunity to clean what no one else wants to clean. She comments, "Not all mothers would spend their vacation cleaning the oven and sorting through the closet."

"I know. Thank you," I reply. "Can we go through the drawers in the dresser now?"

"Can't we take a break?"

"Sure. I'll just wait for you to be ready."

"Can't you relax and just be?"

"Be what?"

"Just be yourself."

She is asking me to be Jen, just Jen. Too often Jen loses herself in what she thinks she is supposed to be and do. I should think of myself as more than a disability. I avoid reflecting on the person I am. Instead I work more or add another volunteer duty to my agenda.

POSSIBILITY

After a morning in my wheelchair, I asked my assistant to transfer me to bed to take the pressure off my butt. After the transfer, she went to the washroom, turning on the radio as she left my room. I heard the hourly newscaster announce that the Supreme Court of Canada had lifted the ban on doctor-assisted suicide. Another option opened to me.

That evening my regular assistant called in sick, so Tom filled in. We lay in bed together.

"How was your day?"

"Did you hear about the Supreme Court decision?" I asked.

He nodded.

"It makes me wonder if it's fair to continue living. It's expensive to maintain me. Dad should have retired years ago but he keeps working in order to afford me. Maybe I should …"

Tom's eyes filled with tears. He leaned in to hug me, nuzzle me with his stubble and kiss me gently on the lips.

"Have you thought about doctor-assisted …?" he asked hesitantly.

I knew if I said yes it would crush him, and his love has meant so much to me.

But the pain of getting dressed and undressed is increasing. I find it harder to convince myself to eat. I'm always tired. I don't think I can take another plane ride to Alberta. I fear last Christmas was my final trip home.

Tom and Jen with Abie, Jen's cat, spring 2015.
(photo courtesy of Snickerdoodle Photography)

Tom hugged me harder.

He continues to hug me.

I know I don't want to ask a doctor to kill me. There is always the possibility of another kiss.

OTHER VOICES

Jamie Simpson

JAMIE SIMPSON, THE FORESTRY coordinator, left EAC to pursue a law degree in 2011. I asked if he had any insights to share from our time working together. He emailed me the following:

Oh, there's a woman in a wheelchair, I thought, in passing, on my way upstairs to my office. We recently had a diversity-in-the-workplace lunch-and-learn. And there was a new diversity policy. Ah, I thought, perhaps this Jen-in-a-wheelchair is part of the Ecology Action Centre's move towards a more diverse staff. And there my thought stopped. Onwards, up the stairs, two at a time, to my office and computer, to tell Nova Scotians about the latest atrocities in our forests. Busy busy. A quick hello. My name's Jamie. My name's Jen. Nice to meet you. See you around. Bye.

But, that woman, whose name is Jen, I remembered, snuck into my brain now and then. Like in the dream I had, where this woman, named Jen, stood up out of her wheelchair to greet me.

Like, when my brain wandered to thoughts of how I define myself. My body that moves. My hands that slip into crevices in rock faces, pulling myself up cliffs. My legs that carry me over twists and turns of forest paths. I thought, what would I be with just my thoughts?

It was Jen who reached out. Hey, Jamie, so do you have a girlfriend? Just curious, because, I hear you don't, and well, I think you might like one of my assistants. Not sure you're her type, but it might be worth checking out.

Who is this woman? I thought.

Our quick beginning-of-the-day hellos became chats. I noticed her clothes, her socks, her skirts. I noticed her wit, her knack for teasing. She asked me about my days, my weekends, my relationship status.

One day she asked, will you carry me up the stairs? The second floor — the boardroom — the place of our staff meetings. It hit me like a falling tree that Jen was excluded from our staff meetings on account of the stairs and lack of elevator. Well, her voice could be at the meetings, through a conference telephone, but not her body, not her face.

Oh, umm, yes, of course I'll carry you, I said, honoured and scared. Careful of my foot, she said as loudly as she could, with concern and trepidation. Yes, yes, of course, your foot, yes, I replied, manoeuvering her with extra care, one arm reaching behind her back, another under her thighs, lifting her up and out of the wheelchair, then, one step at a time, slowly, carefully, up all of the stairs, slowly, step, and another, and another step, and another, and another, and another step, and another. There, there, we're almost there. Just another step.

Hey, said Jen, I hear you're leaving us. And we haven't gone rock climbing or rappelling yet, she said. Right, I said. I had nearly forgotten our dreamed up plan to rig up some sort of contraption to strap Jen to my back and then rappel off of some building together. Was it just a crazy thought? Maybe Jen was just a little hesitant, and maybe I was just a little hesitant. Maybe carrying Jen up the stairs to the second floor, and Jen teasing me about my relationship troubles, and the fondness we had for our morning chats was as far as we were going to go together. Perhaps just the thought of rappelling off of a building together, the possibility we created, that we entertained, envisioning that adventure was enough, or at least far more than we would have guessed at our first passing meeting, when we were just a busy forest campaigner and that new person in a wheelchair.

On my last day at the EAC, Jen had a flower and a bar of fine dark chocolate appear before me. A thought that stopped me, that filled me, with gratitude for our connection.

Brittney Roughan

BRITTNEY ROUGHAN WAS MY assistant for two years during my time at EAC, from 2010 to 2012. She had completed her undergrad at McGill University in Montreal and moved to Halifax with her partner. Brittney and I didn't always see eye-to-eye. She is fastidious. She called me to account when I would speculate or draw conclusions that the data didn't support. I was happy to infer a causal relationship, and she pulled me back. She made me question my own skills, and I often felt tentative and self-conscious because she made me check and check again. She was a challenger but also my ally. Working together was exhausting but the results were worth it. The following is the email she wrote about her experience working with me.

I never knew anyone with a disability before I met Jen. I didn't know how to act at first, but then I realized she was just like me, except her body didn't want to cooperate as much. Sometimes I would forget that she even had a disability. I would get frustrated with her when we would bicker and realized I was mad at her. Then I'd think, "You can't be angry with her," but I realized I could. She didn't get off scot-free because she was disabled. To be mad at her was fine.

At times, I felt really unqualified. Why was I responsible for this person's life? I would think this when Jen would have a spasm and I would have to run and turn off the chair before she went off the edge of the sidewalk, or when she would choke and need sips of tea. I always just kept calm and got her tea, and hoped this wouldn't be the time when the tea didn't work. That was always in the back of my mind. Please, God, don't let me be the one on duty if something bad happens. I had to get to Jen's condo every morning because she depended on me; otherwise she would just be sitting there, alone. It didn't matter if I was hungover, sick or just didn't feel like going in. I couldn't call in sick and have a personal day. I never felt like someone depended on me so much.

I remember when we became friends. Jen was supposed to go to Toronto for a conference and her old roommate bailed on her. She had plane tickets purchased and a hotel booked. She asked me to take her. This would mean twenty-four hours with Jen for four days, constant "work." No breaks. I thought about it. My partner and I were supposed to go to PEI for a mini vacation. But then I realized how much Jen wanted to go, and that I was the only way she was going to be able to go. So I went. And it was fun! It wasn't as intense or as tiring as I thought. We had a great time. We learned a lot.

When Jen got a string of nasty bedsores, I think she trusted me a bit more, or just needed to depend on me. I learned how to use her lift to help her get into bed. I definitely messed that up a few times, but we got through it. That is when I felt Jen was most vulnerable. Here I was, some twenty-something kid, controlling this thing, Jen is hanging from the ceiling and can't even hold her head up, if I didn't hook a strap correctly and she falls... Oh, man. I didn't want to think about that. I was always pretty careful. Jen must have had a lot of faith in me, and all of us, to get her through the day, but then again I guess she didn't have much choice.

Grocery shopping was a bit stressful. Jen was particular about what she wanted. I would try to get the very best descriptions of what she wanted. Stores never have exactly what you want. Sometimes I would just not get a thing if it wasn't the right kind and Jen would be upset. "Why didn't you just pick one? It's not that big of a deal." Other times, I would just get a different kind and Jen still wouldn't be happy. "That's not what I wanted. You shouldn't have gotten anything." It wasn't always like that; sometimes, it would be just fine if I went with my gut feeling.

I learned about patience. I had to. Jen and I would bicker and we would disagree about things. I learned to hold my tongue, but also how to state my view. It was a good lesson in team-work. Sometimes I just wanted to do things my way, or on my own, but we always had to work together. The times Jen would let me work independently were awesome. But then I would realize that I didn't know what I was doing, or how to phrase something. I needed Jen to actually get a lot done. Patience was also a physical thing. Getting from place to place with Jen was sometimes a challenge, but we got pretty efficient at it! I learned a lot about the city, how it's not very accessible. I still comment today when I see places that are not wheelchair friendly. I never really thought about that until I worked with Jen.

I cried during this job more than I have during any other, mostly because I am a sensitive person and react emotionally to criticism or frustrating situations. Sometimes I would go into the bathroom at the EAC, have a bit of a cry, recover, and go back out to work with Jen on whatever it was we were doing. I only cried a couple of times in front of Jen, but she was always really great about it. I'm assuming I'm not the only one who has cried in front of her.

I matured a lot with this job, and learned a lot about Jen and myself. I realized I was a bit of a perfectionist and I don't like being wrong. Working with Jen was humbling, often because I was wrong. But sometimes I was right, and then it was hard to accept that Jen did not think I was right. I had to know I was and move on.

I guess it was a stressful job. Walking out the front of Jen's condo building at 6:00 p.m. was always a liberating feeling. I always let out a sigh of relief. I felt like, "Hey, we got through today. Nothing terrible happened. We got a lot of work done. We had fun. We laughed. Today was a good day."

But sometimes it was a bad day: frustrating, busy or tiring. It was always different. That's what I liked about the job so much. Every day was a new adventure. The last day I walked out of Jen's condo building, I had the greatest sense of relief I've ever felt. I wasn't responsible anymore. But I was also worried. I worried what kid was going to take my place. Could they deal with all the situations I dealt with? Would they get along with Jen like I did? I got over that feeling eventually and realized I wasn't the first full-time assistant she'd ever had. She's done this before, and she'll make it.

Sonya Swift

Sonya Swift worked for me part-time from 2013 to 2014 before she was accepted into medical school at Dalhousie. The following is excerpted from an email she sent me when I asked about her experience working for me.

You opened my eyes to a world that revolves around listening attentively, and critically. You live in the moment more so than anyone else I know — the moment being that split second and also each day for itself. You very rarely miss a thing in a conversation and your memory is such that I catch myself wondering what doesn't get stored inside your head.

You ride a roller coaster of dependence. Some days I would see you and think, "Gosh, Jen is waning..." but then months would pass where I didn't see you and I would come for a visit and I would think, "Gosh, Jen is waxing." I was never continuously struck by your increasing dependence. I was struck by your proactive nature in tackling your future dependence (i.e., the Dynavox). Sometimes you were overly proactive and sold yourself short. Very rarely — honestly, never — did I think to myself, "Jen should have known this was coming/planned for this." It was the extreme opposite thoughts that I had. I don't know if that categorizes you as a "glass half empty" kind of lady... You strike me as quite the opposite but your precautions in planning for your decline were evident to me.

Lessons I will carry:

Jen, you showed me that one is held back only by one's mental conception of an idea. You showed me that ability is a basic (and, perhaps, simplistic) explanation for doing or not doing.

You showed me what hard work looks like.

You proved to me that a dry and witty sense of humour keeps people on their toes, catches them off guard and almost always generates a smile.

Raymond Plourde

THE WILDERNESS COORDINATOR AT the EAC and a member of the Our HRM Alliance team, Raymond Plourde is an experienced environmental advocate who always wore suits to important meetings. I asked him for his thoughts on working with me while I was at the EAC from 2008 to 2013.

I had the pleasure of working with Jennifer Powley on the Our HRM Alliance campaign for several years at the Ecology Action Centre. Everyone loved Jen and so did I. She was so bright and capable and was the undisputed and indefatigable leader of our group, despite the physical limitations brought on by multiple sclerosis. In this sense she was also very inspirational. Small and frail and confined to a wheelchair, she was nevertheless bursting with knowledge, passion and strength. She was impressive in the same way Stephen Hawking was impressive. A lion in a mouse's body. Brilliant, upbeat and determined to be a full participant in society and in life.

At first Jen was able to do presentations and otherwise address a crowd or meeting room verbally, often with galvanizing effect. But over time her energy level began to decline and so did her speaking ability. In my younger years I had worked in radio and listened to a lot of loud rock 'n' roll music and

*attended many loud concerts. As a result I believe I have lost
some of my hearing, particularly in the higher range. So at first I
thought it was just me having a hard time understanding what
Jen was saying in meetings and in casual conversations. But
it eventually became clear that others were also struggling to
hear her. And of course Jen herself was struggling to be heard.
I felt so bad for her. However difficult it was for the rest of us it
must have been tremendously frustrating for Jen. Eventually Jen
decided to leave her job at EAC and return to university. We've
continued on with the work but there is a big hole in our group
now — one that cannot easily be filled.*

Nicole Dodds

MY SISTER NICOLE DODDS and I love each other and have different
opinions on just about everything. She trained as an accountant
but chooses to stay at home with her kids and is a brilliant mother.
She lived in Australia from 2011 to 2016. She sent me her thoughts
after reading an early copy of the manuscript.

*I often get asked, "How's Jen?" Sometimes the answer is, "Her
health is lousy, but she is getting great feedback on her writing."
Sometimes the answer is, "She is working too hard, as usual."
Sometimes the answer is, "Good."*

*In reality I don't always know. Living across the globe has
unfortunately meant that much of what I know about Jen
comes through my mom and I don't know that she always has
the full story. I wish that we were closer, in both senses of the
word.*

*I didn't understand Jen's need to move from Edmonton to
Halifax, and for many years I thought she should move "home,"
especially during her roughest period of anorexia. Now I understand why she stays. Jen's health continues to deteriorate, but
she has an amazing partner in Tom, who makes her very happy.
Jen has an extensive support network of friends and caregivers.*

Jen's life is in Halifax. She has created a wonderful life out of a situation that many could not have handled.

To me, Jen isn't multiple sclerosis. While it makes me incredibly sad to see her body turn against her, and the continual downward progression, I don't think of that when I first think of Jen. I think of a stubborn, opinionated, intelligent, determined woman, who has social activism at the core of her beliefs. I think of the beautiful blonde little girl who used to be my playmate and my rival. I am proud of the way in which she faces the challenges of her daily life and I admire her ability to find pleasure in small things.

Jen's loss of voice is hardest for me. She has always had a sharp tongue and dry sense of humour. While I know her brain still comes up with witty remarks, I feel a loss because she can't say them quickly enough or the moment is lost because she is hard to understand. I never would have imagined missing our banter.

I wish Jen had a closer relationship with Maddie and Ellie. They think of her often. Just today, Ellie asked to purchase a postcard to send to Aunty Jen, completely out of the blue. They love to hear about Jen and me as children. And they hopefully will have a greater appreciation for people with disabilities because of their personal relationship with Jen. But everyone misses out because of the distance between our homes. While that isn't directly a multiple sclerosis thing, Jen's inability to travel means that we can only share Australia with her via stories and photos. I wish she could visit.

I pray for Jen daily, not that she will be miraculously healed — although of course that would be amazing — but that things would be easier for her. Her life is hard. Things that we all take for granted require such effort for her. And I want her to have joy in her life and always know that she is loved by many. I don't know why Jen has multiple sclerosis, but I do know that she has blessed so many people directly and indirectly by the way she has met the challenges of her disease with tenacity and dignity.

Don't get me wrong. She isn't perfect. She can be demanding and cranky. But she is real and that draws people to her, even if at first her physical disability makes them uncomfortable.

How's Jen? She is consistently one of the strongest women I know, in one of the weakest bodies, and I love her more than she will ever know.

Candice Laws

CANDICE LAWS AND I share the same father but have different mothers. We did not grow up in the same household. She now lives in Calgary, Alberta, with her husband Matt. She wrote this letter to me without having seen the manuscript.

You were diagnosed with multiple sclerosis when I was eight. The adults were upset, but beyond that I think it's fair to say I didn't really understand what that meant at the time. As I remember things, this translated to me seeing you more in those first years after your diagnosis than I ever had before. You started to actually be a part of my life. I'm not sure why exactly. Maybe it sparked for you a deeper valuing of family, or maybe you were more easily talked into it because you felt you owed it to our father for the financial support he was providing you. As I write this, I'm not sure why it was, not sure I have ever actually asked.

As the years passed, I watched from a distance how the disease impacted your life. I never appreciated what it actually meant and how it shaped your world. I don't mean to be flip, but it didn't seem like a big deal given it didn't slow you down. When you moved across the country from Alberta to Nova Scotia, I knew it was to establish your independence. This seemed to me normal for someone your age, despite recognizing the motivations you had for doing so were anything but normal. While I saw you more, we rarely spoke. When we did speak, it was superficial. I never knew any different.

Then, something changed. One spring (I am unsure the

year), you came to Calgary for a visit. Your friend and room-mate at the time was travelling here for a conference and you capitalized on the chance to have a buddy that could facilitate you travelling. Just before you were scheduled to return home however, you got sick and ended up in the hospital. Your friend needed to travel back before you were able, raising the question of how you were to get home. You would need a companion and your mother was unable to travel at the time. The added cost of paying for another companion was also discouraging. I took the opportunity to demonstrate that I could help. I arranged for you to access the airlines travel companion program, meaning free companion flights. I then travelled with you back to Halifax.

Until that point, I had not been an active member in your support system. I had spent most of life too far away (figuratively and literally), or too out of the loop to ever be helpful. This forced you to rely on me in a way you never had before. I think in that experience I proved you could rely on me and in that we took the first critical step in building a foundation of trust between us.

This experience changed our relationship entirely. We do more together now. I make a point of visiting you in Halifax, and you make a point of seeing me when you are home in Alberta. I think this started because you came to realize I am here for you and am dependable. I'm not the little girl you used to see me as being. I think it deepened when you grew to trust me enough to open up and share your thoughts on life.

I'm so thankful for this. I am thankful for this because there is no one else in our family I am more alike in my interests and world view. I learn so much from our debates on issues and thoughtful conversations on life. Your sharp wit and (sometime shocking) sense of humor makes me laugh like nothing else. Your stubbornness frustrates me to no end. I cherish it all. I feel we are truly sisters now.

I sometimes wonder if we would have been as close as we are today if it wasn't for this disease you live with. If it wasn't for that turning point in our relationship. I'm frustrated by the fact this thought even crosses my mind. I like to think we would have gotten here regardless. But, still I wonder.

These days, I'm often asked how you are doing, both by those who know you and those you've never met. My response is always the same – you're great! After all, you just completed your second master's degree and are writing your memoirs. You are incredible. A writer. An artist. A community advocate. A sassy, intelligent, woman with the most amazing eyes and an uncanny ability to draw people in and open them up.

When I am honest with myself I know that you are not fine, not physically anyway. The disease you live with is slowly degrading your body, challenging you in everything you do. Now, I really appreciate what that means and how it impacts your life. Now, it impacts mine too because we talk, because it's not just superficial, because I know what it's like to have you as a sister.

WORKS CITED

"Ableism, negative attitudes, stereotypes and stigma." Policy on preventing discrimination based on mental health disabilities and addictions. Canada: Ontario Human Rights Commission, 2014. PDF file.

Burns-Lynch, Bill, Mark S. Salzer, and Richard Baron. *Managing Risk in Community Integration: Promoting the Dignity of Risk and Supporting Personal Choice*. Philadelphia: Temple University Collaborative on Community Inclusion of Individuals with Psychiatric Disabilities, 2011. PDF file.

"Canadians in Context—People with Disabilities." *Indicators of Well-being in Canada*. Canada.ca, 1 Feb. 2016. Web. 11 Mar. 2016.

Chwastiak, Lydia A., and Dawn M. Ehde. "Psychiatric Issues in Multiple Sclerosis." *Psychiatric Clinics of North America* 30.4 (2007): 803-17. *ClinicalKey*. Web. 27 Mar. 2016.

Dalos, Nancy P., et al. "Disease Activity and Emotional State in Multiple Sclerosis." *Annals of Neurology* 13.5 (1983): 573-77. *Wiley Online Library*. Web. 13 July 2016.

Deveau, Leo J. *Nova Scotia Persons with Disabilities Employability Table Discussion Paper: A Review of Identified Employer Concerns for Hiring Persons with Disabilities*. Halifax: The Nova Scotia Persons with Disabilities Employability Table, 2010. PDF file.

D'hooghe, M.B., et al. "Alcohol, coffee, fish, smoking and disease progression in multiple sclerosis." *European Journal of Neurology* 19.4 (2012): 616-24. *Wiley Online Library*. Web. 13 July 2016.

Dyson, Lily L. "Kindergarten Children's Understanding of and Attitudes Toward People With Disabilities." *Topics in Early Childhood Special Education* 25.2 (2005): 95-105. *ClinicalKey*. Web. 27 Mar. 2016.

Federal Disability Report: The Government of Canada's Annual Report on Disability Issues. Gatineau: Human Resources and Skills Development Canada, 2010. PDF file.

Field, Tiffany. "Touch for socioemotional and physical well-being: A review." *Developmental Review* 30.4 (2010): 367-83. *ScienceDirect*. Web. 25 Feb. 2015.

Goodykoontz, Lynne. "Touch: Attitudes and Practice." *Nursing Forum* 18.1 (1979): 4-17. *SAGE*. Web. 12 Dec. 2014.

Livneh, Hanoch. "On the Origins of Negative Attitudes toward People with Disabilities." *Rehabilitation Literature* 43.11-12 (1982): 338-47. Print.

Payne, A. "Nutrition and diet in the clinical management of multiple sclerosis." *Journal of Human Nutrition and Dietetics* 14.5 (2001): 349-57. Print. *Wiley Online Library*. Web. 13 July 2016.

Prince, Michael J. *Pride and Prejudice: The Ambivalence of Canadian Attitudes Toward Disability and Inclusion*. Toronto: Institute for Research and Development on Inclusion and Society, 2009. PDF file.

Rethinking Disability in the Private Sector: We all have abilities. Some are just more apparent than others. Ottawa: Panel on Labour Market Opportunities for Persons with Disabilities, 2013. PDF file.

Saxton, Marsha, et al. "'Bring My Scooter So I Can Leave You:' A Study of Disabled Women Handling Abuse by Personal Assistance Providers." *Violence Against Women* 7.4 (2001): 393-417. *SAGE*. Web. 12 Dec. 2014.

Schwarz, Stefan, and Hans Leweling. "Multiple sclerosis and nutrition." *Multiple Sclerosis* 11.1 (2005): 24-32. *SAGE*. Web. 27 Mar. 2016.

Simpson, Robert J., et al. "Physical and mental health comorbidity is common in people with multiple sclerosis: nationally representative cross-sectional population database analysis." *BMC Neurology* 14.128 (2014): 1-8. *BioMed Central*. Web. 13 July 2016.

Terzi, Murat, et al. "The Eating Disorders in Multiple Sclerosis Patients." *Journal of Neurological Sciences (Turkish)* 26.3 (2009): 311-17. *Journal of Neurological Sciences (Turkish)*. Web. 13 July 2016.

Timmerman, Gayle M., and Alexa K. Stuifbergen. "Eating Patterns in Women with Multiple Sclerosis." *Journal of Neuroscience Nursing* 31.3 (1999): 152-58. Print.

The History of Attitudes to Disabled People: Disability Fossilized in Myths, Literature, Theatre, Folklore, Biography and History. n.p., Feb. 2007. Web. 13 July 2016.